GETTING WHAT YOU WANT

Have you ever wanted something and gotten something else, a substitute? The more we get used to substitutes, the more we deny ourselves what we really want. We don't get to marry the one we really want, so we marry a substitute. We don't have enough money for lobster at dinner, so we have tuna. Our lives are full of substitutes. You get what you choose, and if you think in terms of substitutes, you become accustomed to saying things like "Oh, it doesn't matter. I'll have whatever."

Go for what you want—you don't have to have a substitute or sell out. You can have what you want. Having what you want is being wealthy. Being wealthy isn't being extravagant or wasteful, it's having exactly what you want.

How to Have
More In a
Have-Not World

Terry Cole-Whittaker

FAWCETT CREST • NEW YORK

A Fawcett Crest Book
Published by Ballantine Books

Library of Congress Catalog Card Number: 83-42625

ISBN 0-449-20673-4

This edition published by arrangement with Rawson Associates

Manufactured in the United States of America

First Ballantine Books Edition: April 1985

I dedicate this book to you, my former husband, Leonard. I am eternally grateful for the opportunity for us to have been together and to have assisted each other through our mutual love and support into a greater experience of God. The Holy Spirit brought us together for our healing, and when it was complete at that level of awareness we were released into a new life. No one can separate what God has brought together; we are always one just as all beings are one in God.

Contents

Don't Worry; It's Working!

The Sweet Life—Now

Acknowledgments

No one does anything alone. It is my experience that God's love is all and that each of us is a cell in the body of God, working together for the glory and pleasure of God.

I especially appreciate and publicly acknowledge the following beings for their contribution to my life and the work that I do: my former husband, Leonard; my daughters, Suzanne and Rebecca; our son-in-law and Rebecca's husband, David Wiesehan; my parents, Adam Reich, Barbara Crawford; my other family members; and the staff and volunteers in the ministry, whose love, commitment, and dedication make it all happen. There are also those teachers I have been privileged to know, whose books I have read, whose courses I have taken, and through whom I have experienced God's love and truth, and I especially want to acknowledge them.

Jesus of Nazareth is my savior and my guide to the Holy Spirit. The wisdom and teachings of Lao-Tzu and Buddha have also been a gift of God to me.

Ernest Holmes brought me to the principle of life and taught me about who I am. The Course in Miracles is a constant source of love and truth for me.

I acknowledge all those who came before me whose courage and vision as expressed through themselves and their work have brought us spiritually closer to our divine potential. I acknowledge the gnostics, metaphysicians, pentecostals, Martin Luther, Moses, quantum physics, Sigmund Freud, Ida Rolf, Rebirthing, nutrition, exercise, Oral Roberts, the Reverend Ike, Werner Erhard, L. Ron Hubbard, Robert Panté, Marshall Thurber, Bhagwan Rajneesh, Sondra Ray, Fritz Perls, William James, Abraham Maslow, Jamie Weinstein, Bel Evans, and Yoga. Also the believers, the doubters, and the skeptics, as well as all others I know of and don't know of who have and are contributing to my life and the lives of others. I salute each of you, and I am deeply grateful to you.

I thank Eleanor and Ken Rawson, my publishers; Elizabeth Backman; Neale Marshall-Walsch; Dixie, the typist; and, Cheryl Rosoff, for working with me to get this book completed, published, and distributed to you. It's all working.

Thanks!

****

You've Got What It Takes!

****

* 1 *

How to Have More in a Have-Not World

You can have exactly what you want, when you want it, all the time. There are people for whom this is true, and they become better off every day. These people are rare, and it's possible you've never even met one. If you are one of them, this book will assist you in becoming even more of what you are capable of being. If you are not, this book will provide the opportunity for you to be, do, and have exactly what you want and to become a happier and more loving person.

This may sound unrealistic, but there is that part of you that wants what I've said to be true. Listen to that part of you, for that is your heart and intuition speaking. Just about everyone has what it takes to be, do, and have what they want. This book is written for those of you who are willing and courageous enough to reach out for it all.

This isn't a get-rich-quick scheme. This is not some easy way to turn straw into gold. It will take time, your commitment, courage, and willingness along with hard work and persistence.

There always have been people who have the material possessions they want, the symbols of success they have striven for, whether it be fame, power, or riches. There are many who have wonderful loving relationships, healthy bodies, and a positive attitude. There are also those who experience and feel the presence of a higher power.

Don't go for "bits and pieces." What I'm talking about is having all you truly desire within a context or a framework of self-fulfillment and satisfaction. Too many people go for bits and pieces of the pie of life, never really dreaming that they can have it all. Having it all doesn't mean compromising and selling out in order to get it. Having it all goes beyond the first rush of a new love, beyond the momentary thrill you get from winning a race, buying a stereo or a new car, or getting a promotion at work. Having is an attitude that goes beyond the material world and transcends the conditions and events of your life. Having even transcends attitude. It is a direct result of knowing who you are and living your life from that realization.

The Two Parts of *Having*

There are two parts to having. *The first part deals with you the person as a producer or generator of your life*. This is the key. Without this all the effort and struggle will get you nowhere, but with the key, struggle is unnecessary. You are the one who actually says how your life will be, and it's you who imagines it into actuality.

The second part is the mastery of life itself. To master

something is to own it. When you know the principles of life, you will also learn the rules of life and how to use them consistently to produce the results you desire. Talk is cheap and so are ideas. Making those ideas happen is where the power is. There are plenty of good people who wish, hope, try, and desperately want to have, but who stop right there and do not make the effort to implement their dreams. To have in a have-not world requires that you know who you are and be a master at playing the game of life.

There are unwritten laws of life. If you don't know this and don't use them consciously, life at its best is the worst of what it could be. You might know in your heart that you are really a great pianist, but you don't play the piano because you don't know how. To develop under these circumstances takes both knowing that you are potentially a magnificent pianist, even when you begin your lessons, and a lot of dedication. As you play the piano with commitment, you eventually learn to play at the level of expertise that you always knew you would. *Your results are aligned with your awareness*. This takes commitment and practice. You have to work at it—and you have to believe.

If you have neither the awareness of who you are, nor the developed skills and knowledge to produce the results you want, you are in deep trouble. Life at that level is a huge struggle, filled with frustration, discouragement, resentment, accidents, and more. To master life is to transcend *life*, so that you can experience *living*. There is a difference, as we will see.

In my life I become more aware every day of who I am and of the power that flows through me. I also become more skilled in the use of my talents and committed to doing what I say I will, thus having what I want *consistently*. Life is not now and never was a game of chance, as far as I am concerned. Life has law and order, and the sun shines on all of us alike, though you may be standing in the shade wondering why it's cold and dark. Only you can move you, by an act of will, out into the light. Out of that conscious act of will the forces of life align with you in your new purpose and intention. Those who "have" are those who move themselves; they know that it's up to them. There is no one out there who will lead you by the hand. You have to count on yourself to motivate yourself.

We live in a have-not world. The vast majority of the population of this earth, at least 95 percent, live as victims or potential victims of forces they believe are outside of themselves. Most people are waiting for something outside of themselves to move them, save them, or do it for them. We give power to events, other people, things, conditions, and places instead of placing the responsibility on ourselves. To be ignorant of who you are and the basic laws of life is to flounder and to be a passenger or bystander rather than an active participant. The more you *increase* the power the world has over you, the more you *decrease* the power you have over the world. In the Book of Genesis in the Bible there is a verse that says that God gave us dominion over the earth. It didn't give earth power over us. Yes, there are the laws of nature that we need to know and live with. The human being has the added dimension of conscious choice and will.

A master learns the rules. You can choose whether or not to master life and experience living fully. It's up to you. To master anything you must know the rules, how they function, how to use them, and what you want them to do for you. Master skiers do not make up their own rules; they discover what works in skiing. They become one with their skis, the mountain, and the snow. A true master skier loses herself in the skiing as a master dancer loses himself in the dance. The effort disappears, and what is left is the experience of effortlessness. It's like a moment of ecstasy between lovers—you as individuals disappear and what is left is holy communion. A master through his/her dedication loses separate identity and becomes the experience of cosmic energy in motion. *It takes effort to become effortless.* The rules of life apply to all of life, so you don't have to figure everything out. Discover the basics and they apply in every part of your life. It just looks complicated.

A master uses Life. The spirit and the body appear to be in direct opposition, for one is infinite, immortal, and absolute, and the other is finite, temporary, and relative. The apparent conflict is what needs to be addressed. In the Gospel of John, the Bible says, "The Spirit is willing but the flesh is weak." There seems to be a direct conflict between who you are as a being, and the spirit in your body or the physical.

The challenge is to have your flesh become servant to <
your spirit. You learn the laws and the way of the physical and, through a marriage of sorts, your being or self is champion. The seeming conflict between man and nature disappears into a union and celebration of life. The physical world becomes your tool, it becomes your playground. For most people the physical world is their burden and their downfall. Their spirit becomes slave to their flesh. To be a master is to use your medium of self-expression as a singer uses breath and vocal cords and the artist uses canvas and paint and brushes. Life is to be used.

A master knows not fear. Life is not mysterious; we hide *ourselves* from life, then we pretend that some disturbing aspects of life, including ourselves, are mysterious. Because we've already labeled a huge part of life mysterious and frightening, it's even more frightening to confront what you fear. Some people handle fear by retreating more and more, creating for themselves more imagined safety by protecting themselves, hiding out, building up defenses and offenses, all the while becoming less powerful under the illusion of safety.

The more you fear life and the world, the less freedom you have and the less opportunity you have to enjoy the love, ecstasy, and celebration that comes from mastery. The truth is that there is no danger; it is your defenses that are creating the enemy. When you serve your fear you actually create monsters. Some retreat; some, instead of retreating, become more militaristic and power mad. Some even try to prevent loss, hurt, and pain by armoring themselves with wealth, power, and fame. The way of the world doesn't work and only leads to less joy and happiness and more fear and isolation.

A master moves toward the power. Diminishing yourself or overcompensating for believing you are not enough are both expressions of powerlessness. The closer to zero power you get, the more complex, confusing, and threatening life becomes. The closer to zero you become, the more you lose your identity and the more you attach yourself to the world and its symbols. You then believe and experience yourself to be temporary and destructable and essentially powerless. The world looms large, and the challenge of life seems bigger than you are.

The closer to infinite power you become, the more simple, clear, and supportive life becomes. When you realize who you are, you continue to expand to higher levels of awareness and power, or the infinite; and the things, events, conditions, beliefs, and emotions move downward, where they belong, toward zero, where they have less and less power over you. See it this way: The higher you go, the more effortless and joyful life and living are. At this level you want to live forever and life for you is a banquet.

Resolving the Conflict

A primary conflict within us is the one that arises out of being torn between the spiritual and the physical. The further away you go from the spiritual, the closer you draw to the physical. You become an inanimate, temporary, terminal person. To move away from this you must shift the way you perceive, experience, and realize yourself. You must take back the power you have transferred to inanimate objects, other people, places, things, experiences, decisions, beliefs, emotions, thoughts, and values. You must become the self that holds it all, being held by God or what you may choose to call a higher power. You must be as spirit, forever expanding into higher levels of awareness and living.

The downward process occurs when a person *assumes that he or she is only a body with a name*. The process of "not having" begins early, and every decision you make to the effect that "you can't have" moves you a step closer to zero. Every decision you make to the effect "I can have what I want" moves you a step closer to living as a whole, complete, and alive human being. To wake up from the nightmare is to see yourself clearly for the first time.

"Things" don't mean anything. If people are not *awake and aware*, their lives are about their money, jobs, clothes, others' opinions, cars, sex, righteousness, as well as about their bodies, the neighbors, the government, age, houses, the past, the future, who's wrong, luck—you name it.

Life and living are two distinct parts of life. When you confuse the essence of *life* with *living*, you stop living and your life becomes a matter of going through the motions of pushing, pulling, changing, moving, hiding, losing, finding, wanting, and not wanting the essence. Material things are just that and no more. *Things* don't mean anything. Life doesn't mean anything, it just is. *You* are the meaning, the value. When you ride on the crest of this wave, all of life, its happenings, and surprises work for you.

Renouncing life and "things" is not the answer. To renounce the World and the game itself doesn't solve anything, and you miss the point. It would be the same as avoiding an intimate relationship because you don't want to be hurt or to hurt. You renounce relationship, believing that you are now free. You're not free, you are still being controlled by your fears and belief system, and you are still alone. The sweetness of life comes from being fully *in* it, but not *consumed* by it. A truly courageous person is the one who throws him- or herself with abandon into life.

To renounce is to confirm that the power of the physical world and your fears and negative emotions are greater than you are. *You are only truly free when to have or not have are choices made from an awareness of "I can have what I want."*

TO FEAST OR FAST IS NOT IT

If you feel like renouncing something, get more into what you are renouncing, so you can experience and discover what your attachment to it is, and then you will let it go naturally. To feast totally is as transforming as to fast totally. To feast or fast is not a way of life or an end in itself. Nothing is significant or important in itself. It is all merely a stage setting or a vehicle or tool for self-realization. To actualize and realize the self is to live freely, not bounded by the self-imposed limitations of the mind. To actualize the self is to be able to draw upon your inner resources, your unused talents and abilities for a life of total participation, fulfillment, and love.

Look at the power and the opportunity you gain in living unencumbered by the weight of limiting beliefs of the past. Just imagine what is possible for you. Too few people realize that life is not to be tolerated or put up with, but to be lived freely as one chooses. *Life* is external; true *living* occurs internally.

To be caught up in *life* rather than in *living* is to miss the purpose of living. The world is full of damaged people who maintain their lives at various levels of survival, who have missed living. No one is to be condemned or even blamed for not living, but it is time for all of us to awake to all the possibilities we are missing. Many people live in a condition of false hope or hopelessness. People who live in false hope are waiting to be saved; they are waiting for an answer or a sign. They are waiting for someone to tell them what to do and for someone or something outside of themselves to give them what they want and need. Too many people go downhill waiting for an answer.

Years ago I used to wait for the newspaper every morning so that I could read my astrology sign for the day, to see if this was "the day." Of course it never was until I stopped waiting for an answer and took action, sign or no sign. (Then *every day* became "the day.")

I lived in hope and hopelessness, feeling a victim of my circumstances and the people around me until I woke up. There are still times every now and then when I go back into my old patterns, especially when I'm reaching out into unknown territories and new levels of participation and commitment in my personal and business life. My tendency is to blame others and feel that I'm not appreciated or acknowledged after all I did for them—this little racket of mine still appears. But I now recognize it much more quickly and let it go much faster as I see what it costs me to use it in my life. When I see a problem or a seeming obstacle, I expand myself and my purpose to include that problem being solved and that obstacle being handled in such a way that everyone wins.

Getting to the Turning Point

What it takes to have and to be a having person is to wake up and restore yourself to who you are step by step. People cannot really be damaged, unless they choose to remain damaged once they've awakened. Waking up is becoming more conscious and more aware. To be asleep, as mentioned in the Bible and some famous legends and tales, is not to know, not to experience.

The true turning point comes when a person awakens as if from a deep sleep and sees and hears everything as if for the first time. *Transformation occurs at this point.* It is as if you were reborn, a fresh birth into a new world. This time it is a world of life and you are the cause of your life. The real turnabout happens when you surrender to God. True union with the higher power takes away all fear and replaces it with peace. Peace and love become the desire of the heart of a whole person.

THE ROLE OF LOVE

A person is damaged when denied love. To be denied love is to be denied beingness and value. To be denied beingness or beinghood makes us a nonentity, puts us down to zero. This usually happens early on in our childhood, and it can continue throughout our lifetime if we don't stop this process by turning our lives around. To turn around and go in the opposite direction is to repent; it is to go home or back to your natural state of being. Your natural state of being is that of a spiritual entity that is whole, complete, and perfect. Wholeness is a state of awareness; it is an attitude, a ground of being. The truth is that you are always whole, complete, and perfect whether you want to accept it or not.

Beingness is a natural result of love and acceptance. *Acceptance is the first level of love.* If you don't know what love is, start by accepting yourself as you are without the desire to change. This in itself is a huge step and the most important one. Nothing restores a person as does love. Love is all. Love heals all. Love is complete in and of itself. Love is the purpose, the goal, and the path to the fulfillment of itself.

Love and acceptance imply ability and trust. To be stopped, forced, or given something that is a substitute for what you really want denies love, trust, and beingness. Our *natural* inclination is to express, to create, and to assert ourselves into life.

Add up all the times you were stopped or felt you were repressed in some way. You could be suffering from a major blockage that actually is stopping you today. To remove the blockage, you must see it and realize the impact it has had on you, and finally, be willing to express your anger if need be and to let the past go and get on with living.

* *Look into your life and recall the times you were stopped from being, doing, and having what you wanted.*

* *Reexperience what that was like and how you felt and the decisions you made out of those events.*

* *Ask yourself, What impact are those decisions from yesterday making in my life today?*

When you are stopped, especially when it's important to you, you may give up going for what you want. Or you may sneak around and lie to get it. Or you may try and stop others from being, doing, and having what they want. Being stopped represses us, and if not seen for what it is and transcended, destroys our will and breaks our spirit. When we feel that we have been stopped or repressed, we feel helpless and immobilized, stuck and unable. You can only *stop* yourself.

Being forced to do what you don't want to do also can diminish you. If we are bullied, threatened, and forced, we become weak, confused, timid, and fearful; some of us may even use threats and force to get what we want. To be forced to be, do, or have what you don't want builds incredible anger, resentment, and hostility. Authority figures become enemies and a potential threat to our well-being. At some levels we have all allowed such a state of mind to happen to us, but what is more important is that you can regain your power yourself. To regain your power, you need to realize the impact of this condition on your life and be willing to let it go. Only we can restore ourselves.

* *Recall if you were ever forced to be, do, or have what you didn't want.*

* *Allow yourself to experience what occurred, how you felt, and the decisions you made.*

* *Ask, How do those situations affect my life today?*

* *Ask yourself, Do I treat people that way; am I still feeling forced beyond my control?*

If you rebel against anything that looks like force, and therefore force or the fear of force is running your life, you create your own monsters out of your fears and belief systems.

Getting What You Want

Have you ever wanted something and got something else, a substitute? The more we get used to substitutes, the more we deny ourselves what we really want. We don't get to marry the one we really want, so we marry a substitute. We don't have enough money for lobster at dinner, so we have tuna. Our lives are full of substitutes. You get what you choose, and if you think in terms of substitutes, you become accustomed to saying things like, "Oh, it doesn't matter, I'll have whatever," or "That's fine—it's good enough for me." You want butter and you have butter substitute. You want love and you take a kick in the pants. You want to be alive and you settle for half a life, for being half dead.

Go for what you want—you don't have to have a substitute or sell out. You can have what you want. Having what you want is being wealthy. Being wealthy isn't being extravagant or wasteful, it's having exactly what you want. To have more than you want is a statement of scarcity, just as is not having enough. Instead of going to a restaurant and ordering a whole dinner simply to justify having the dessert, forget the main course and order only the dessert.

To be stopped, forced, or given a substitute all contribute to our losing faith in ourselves, God, and life. Life is a marvelous adventure, and deep within our hearts we want to play the game full out. Stop battling, resenting, or trying to get even. Heal yourself and have what you want. Why resist so hard? Instead, see obstacles for what they are— an opportunity for you to be greater than they are. You actually can use those obstacles to *help* achieve your goals and objectives. (We will dwell on that in more detail in a later chapter.)

Choose to be alive. Most people never question their lives other than with a "Why me, God?" Look into people's faces; see how many are alive, happy, vital people who are turned on and living their vision. Notice that most people—the average people—are half dead. The sparkle and the glow is gone. They are asleep, the sleep is getting deeper, and the worst part is that they don't realize it.

It's not wrong to be asleep, it's just that all the goodies of life are for those who are awake. Recall how inspiring it is to be around a fully alive person. An awake person ignites the fire of passion within people's hearts. In order for us to awaken to who we are and to the passions of life within ourselves, we must first realize that we have been asleep.

Choose to drop your "act." The walking dead all too often pretend to themselves and others, for the sake of seeming okay, that they are just fine. To be unaware that you are unaware is ignorance at its most destructive level. Pretense can be so much a part of a person's life that he or she doesn't even realize it. The desire to keep up a front becomes a way of life. When you are your act, when you are your problems, you can't step back and see yourself. But you have the power to change!

Choose to tell the truth. It takes a tremendous amount of courage for someone to wake up, because it requires telling the truth, possibly for the first time. Others often don't want to hear that truth, because deep down inside they know it's their truth also. They believe they have too much at stake in their act to risk the loss of the false security and comfort it gives them. Those are the very things you need to be willing to lose. To become more alive, more powerful, and closer to living as you choose in this world, you have a lot to face and deal with. When your security is attached to the people, places, things, beliefs, and concepts of yesterday, you cannot be free to be who you are today. That which is yours today will be with you, that which isn't will fall away. True power comes from being fully *in* life and not *of* life.

THE FEAR OF BEING POWERFUL

A fear of being powerful often keeps people damaged and powerless. Look beneath the surface and into the cause of powerlessness and you will discover what has held you back. The fear of being, doing, and having it all is the key issue.

There is a fear of having too much good, too much happiness, too much health, too much wealth, too much love, and basically too much life. Most people would say, "Sure, I'm willing, but they are not!" Part of that fear may be the thought that you can't be trusted and would misuse, waste, or be irresponsible if you have unlimited quantities of whatever it is that you desire.

Other thoughts that could hold you back are that you don't deserve it or perhaps that it isn't spiritual or right to have that much pleasure and good. There is a taboo against pleasure, the same taboo against having that makes this a pleasureless, have-not existence for most people. But it doesn't have to be! You can have it all.

Let's get it straight about power. We've all seen and experienced the misuse of power, and we've all made decisions about power—including whether it is good or bad, right or wrong. It isn't that power is good or bad; it is that people misuse power. It isn't even that people are good or bad; it's their beliefs about themselves. If you believe you are worthless, so are others and so is life. You are worth it! Power is power, just as money is money. It is neutral. It just *is*. People attribute meaning to power, and people use or misuse the energy power generates. But people basically are good—a much-guarded secret. So it is time we freed ourselves to be who and what we are. To be restored, we have to begin by realizing we are not our thoughts, we are not our labels, we are not our past.

Get it straight about love, too. We can't live in the present in love and peace by referring to what our past tells us about love. Your past doesn't know about love. Love is in the present. It is the essence of life. It isn't a memory; it can't be stored, stockpiled, or bought. Love fills all space and time with itself. If you have experienced pain and loss in love in some form or another, you have been damaged. Love at these moments seemed nonexistent. Pain and loss can be threats to our physical and emotional survival. Life becomes a losing proposition instead of a celebration of love and creation.

Let's get it straight about loss. Loss doesn't exist, it is merely an *evaluation* of a condition or event of some kind. I'm not saying we can't be hurt physically, but I'm saying that each painful event, unless released, becomes another opportunity to shut down, shut off, and turn off. Some people become more violent and strike out as a way to prevent more hurt and loss, while others flee, either physically or emotionally. The key here is that you can let go of the impact of the pain and loss and come back fully to your power and love. The damage resides in your memory bank as well as in the tissues of your body. What is needed is for you to release and cast off what isn't necessary mentally and physically in order to be restored. Let go. The damage can only remain if you hold on to it, using it and choosing to be damaged. There is no redeeming value in being damaged.

A GAME WE'VE ALL PLAYED

When I was a teenager, we used to play a game that left a big impression on me. We'd ask a person who never played the game before to sit on the floor and then would cover them with a blanket. We'd then tell them that they had something on their body, something they were wearing, that they didn't need. They were then asked to throw the unneeded article out on the floor. What was so amazing is that people would take off their clothes or their jewelry, not realizing the thing they didn't need was the blanket.

We search and search looking for answers, not realizing the obvious. We don't *need* the pain and loss. We actually use it, and billions thrive on it. Some people are so repressed and shut down that the only time they feel alive is when they hurt. So to feel alive they create upset, drama, and pain just to experience something. Something always looks better than nothing. Here we must fight fire with fire, and know that the way *out* is the way *through*. To give up pain and loss, we have to be willing to experience them if necessary and then give up the value we imagine there is in keeping them. Unless fully experienced and released, emotional pain will stay with us at some level incessantly.

Overcoming Denial

Pain is directly related either to physical or emotional trauma. Physical traumas—accidents, illnesses—often are preceded by emotional trauma directly related to our relationship with others. There appear to be two opposing energy flows within us. One is our desire and need to love and be loved by others, and the other is to attain autonomy, spiritual wholeness, and self-sufficiency. These forces seem to be in conflict, and yet they are coexistent and necessary. What is needed is to know the law and to allow the mental to surrender to the spirit. The challenge is "to be in the world and not of it." The challenge is to surrender totally into love and live, being responsible for and the cause of your life at the same time.

Giving our power away can take us in a downward spiral. But we *can* turn around through an act of will. To have what you want during an apparent downward spiral, you must recognize that no one is stopping you, suppressing you, or holding you down. Your power is in your own hands.

Let's get it straight about denial. No one denies you anything—life denies you nothing; in fact, it is there for you in its fullest. Denial is not real, it is an illusion. The Universe only says yes, it never says no. Because you may not have what you want or be burdened with what you don't want, it appears that others or life deny you. The big block against having what you want is the idea that *no* is an option. *No* doesn't exist. *Yes* is the ultimate permission, and you must accept that you have that permission and go for it all.

I'm not saying you need to say yes to everything. It's absolutely right for you to say no. Your saying no makes for clarity as to what you want and defines your yesses. It's that life only says yes. The no's are yours.

Since no one denies you anything, what do you want? What are you willing to be, do, and have? *To believe you are denied life is to blame, resent, and deny yourself and others even more. Affirm life and life affirms you.* You will have to work to let go of your old way of being and seeing the world. The old way you had of viewing life, people, events, and opportunities will no longer work for you. It's a constant process of choosing and selecting what supports you and your vision at each new level of your growth and awakening. Consider these points and take these steps to affirming yourself.

* *Life is a hologram, that is, you can look at any part and see the whole. Your relationship with yourself is recreated everywhere in your life.*

* *Every cell in your body contains the entire story of your body. The microcosm is a smaller version of the macrocosm.*

* *Look at your relationship to money and you can discover the relationship you have with God. (You may think this is strange, and you don't have to believe me. Just start looking.) Money is our energy flow and a symbol of acknowledgment and wealth.*

* *Look at your relationship to wealth. Life is a mirror for each of us, and by using that mirror you can discover yourself, and in that process life opens itself up to you and passes out so many blessings that you couldn't possibly hold them all.*

It is necessary for you to bring forth that which is within you. That which is within you is unlimited and without form until you, through your imagination, call forth and bring into existence what you want. To be aware of this process is to be empowered.

The fortunate among us are those who live out on the edge of life, creating out of their imagination, unlimited by their past, beliefs, concepts, and the world they see and know. For me it is God that lives through me; I must allow myself to be a clean and clear pipeline and vehicle for that power to express itself through me. That means I must first get out of my own way and clear the way for what is mine.

Living Your Vision

This book is about your living your vision. What is a vision? I call a vision that which inspires you, motivates you, and turns you on to life. Your vision is your special way, the way in which you want to express yourself and contribute to the quality of other people's lives at the same time. What is it that you've always wanted to do? Where is it that you know you could make a contribution to others' lives? What is of great importance to you? *That is your vision. Do that.*

I have discovered that everyone has a deep commitment and burning desire to give to others, to assist others, and to make this world be the heaven that it can be. For some that vision is clear and they are living it, step by step. They have a purpose and a commitment that is greater than themselves.

To draw upon your greatness, you must have a great and worthwhile purpose. Otherwise you stay small, petty, and painfully boring. Unless you unlock your greatness, the only people around you will be those who seem to have an undying commitment to the trivia of their latest ailment, their relationship problems, and their victim stories in the form of "I said, and she said, and I said, and then she said," along with a generous sprinkling of "Isn't it awful?" "When is somebody going to do something?" and the "Things are getting worse, woe is me" blues.

Your life depends on this. Living your vision is rediscovering (if you haven't already) what it is you've always wanted to do. When you take your natural talents, which may not seem like much to you, and combine them with a commitment to use those talents to enrich, inspire, empower, and transform other people's lives and the quality of all life, you have the key to paradise. What could be greater than loving and being loved and doing work, whether as a volunteer or a professional, that is your dream? All you've ever wanted to do is give, contribute, and help people. If you've failed or been shut down in some way, even ridiculed and laughed at, you may have deeply hidden your vision beneath the hurt and pain, swearing never again to let it be known. Your life depends on your finding your vision again.

PASSION, PERSISTENCE, AND COMMITMENT

To live your vision fully is to live with passion as a life partner. Living is empty without passion. Passion is your vital energy enlisting the support of your heart and soul for a great work. Combine that passion with persistence and commitment, and the world is yours. You then gain more than the world; you gain your relationship to life, to God, to love, and to your soul, all of which makes the gifts of the world pale in comparison. Everyone must be in love, for without love and passion you are a stick impersonating a person. To be alive you must be willing to savor fully every morsel of life, you must become an open being always willing to discover what's next.

My commitment lies in providing this book for those of you who have and want more *and* for those of you who don't but are willing to. How to have more in a have-not world requires that you declare yourself one of the chosen ones simply because *you* have chosen. The rest of this book is actually about that as a restoration process.

Use the exercises and techniques at the end of each of the chapters in this book as support tools to assist you in applying the information and getting the results you desire.

You can use them over and over as each new challenge places a demand on you to move to a higher level of awareness, love, and mastery. They will assist you in discovering your wants, your vision, and your blockages to being, doing, and having what you choose. Through the use of these exercises, you can clear yourself of obstacles and open yourself to living the loving, wealthy, and peaceful life that is available to you.

Exercises

WHAT DO YOU WANT?

1. Move through any uncomfortableness and write down exactly what you want. Be specific. This is the first question in any situation and the basic one in life. Answering it is a must. Are you willing to have that much good?

"HAVING" EXERCISES

2. Do these every day until you feel restored.

   * Practice looking at things and qualities of life and say, "I can have that." Also say, "That's for me."

   * Be aware and conscious of your body, your feelings, your reactions, and your experience from moment to moment.

   * Notice where you are. Look around and see details as well as the overview. People allow themselves to be diminished by other people and things. Reverse the tendency by paying attention to and observing people, surroundings, events. You take the fear and mystery out of what you directly, carefully observe.

* Look at people, situations, events, and materials and see them for what they actually are, not for what you think they mean or have represented to you in the past.

* Use these statements and notice your reaction: "The world I see doesn't mean anything," then, "I give the meaning to what I see."

RESTORATIVE EXERCISES

3. Write down any and all failures you've had with a bearing on purposes, goals, wants, dreams, relationships, etc.

4. Select the purposes, goals, wants, and dreams you desire even if you've failed at them before. Recover your life by recovering your purposes, objectives, intentions, and vision.

5. Identify any events in your life wherein you felt stopped, diminished, or powerless. Did you as a result of any incident shut yourself down and decide to be less than you are? Or did you decide to make others less so they couldn't overpower you?

6. Look at what it's cost you to shut down and realize the decisions you made as a result of shutting down and their impact on your life.

7. Who stopped you, forced you, or gave you substitutes for what you really wanted? What have you done to get even, shut down, get what you want, etc?

8. Write down any thoughts, fears, beliefs, and notions that have to do with you and others having exactly what you/they want.

CREATION

9. Close your eyes and allow yourself to see, sense, and feel yourself in your ideal scene. See yourself having what you want in detail. Allow yourself to "mock it up" in your imagination, envisioning your future experience. Make it real! Do this once or twice a day, as wanted.

10. Write these affirmative statements about your having what you want ten times per day for one week. If any doubts, fears, or misgivings come forth from within you, simply write them out in the margin of the page. Then write the affirmative statement again and continue on. Remember, you are creating afresh, and these affirmations may be difficult to accept at first. Keep on.

* It is okay for me, (_____), to have exactly what I want!

* I, (_____), can have what I want.

* Everything in life is here for me, (_____), to enjoy.

* The more powerful I am, the more loving I am.

* Everyone is happy that I, (_____), was born and am fully alive and living my vision.

* 2 *

Trust in Yourself—
You Are Enough

No one can make decisions for you, no one can tell you
what you should want or do, and no one but you can be
responsible for you or determine the quality of your life.
The big questions are:

* Do you trust yourself with the responsibility for your
  life?

* Do you trust yourself with that much power?

* Are you able to make the right choices and to take
  care of yourself?

The main concern of most of us is: Did I, can I now,
and will I do it right? The second big concern is: Where
am I going to get what I need, where will it come from,
and where will it go?

The answer to the first concern is "yes"; the answer to the second concern is "from yourself and to yourself." The trust is that you have everything you want and need just waiting to be called forth into action. The truth also is that you are perfectly trustworthy and able to take care of yourself and of all people on this planet, if you choose to contribute yourself at that vast level.

To realize yourself at this level and to trust in trusting yourself is a process of perpetual discovery. What you discover is that a miracle happens out of the realization that you are the only one you can trust and count on—you then find you can trust and count on others. It's putting the horse before the cart, where it belongs. When you use another person to hide behind, who lives your life for you, it doesn't work. When you are in charge, then everyone and everything becomes a lesson, a love experience, and/or a contribution.

You will not find what you are looking for outside yourself. This is great news—you don't have to seek far and wide for what you need and want. You have it all right now. I used to hear that, and while I knew it was true at some level, other than that faint flicker of truth, I didn't have a clue as to where to look, how to look, or even how to draw upon this great reservoir of wisdom, knowledge, and love.

Understanding the Issue of Trust

The fundamental issue in this chapter is trust, self-trust. Without being able to depend upon yourself, you cannot have what you want. You won't even trust that what you want is what you *want*. The first stepping-stone in having what you want is first to ask, "What *do* I want?" If you say, "I don't know," then whom are you going to ask? Who does know? It isn't that most people aren't able to get what they want; it's that few people have ever been intimate with themselves and allowed themselves to fully experience all that is available to them from within themselves. Without this conscious personal relationship with ourselves, we have to look elsewhere for what we believe we need. *Life then becomes a constant search for what you believe yourself to be missing.*

THE DANGER OF NOT TRUSTING LIFE

Lack of self-trust is self-invalidation. The problem is that self-doubt does not lead to self-trust; you just doubt yourself more. To reverse that downward spiral, begin by trusting yourself. It sounds difficult to ask you to trust yourself when you start out not trusting yourself. It's like not being able to get a job until you have experience, but you can't get experience unless you have a job. You start from being there; you start with positive action in the direction in which you want to go. *You trust by trusting.*

Trusting yourself is actually trusting life, since you are part of nature and life. You have one with all life, and that oneness implies that you're everywhere present, all knowing and all powerful. The outermost part of the universe is the innermost part of you. You are a part of all life, and all of life is a part of you. What is known anywhere is known within you, and whatever is going on with you is felt at every point in the universe.

In the movie *Star Wars*, Obi Wan-Kenobi talked about feeling a shift in the Force—that was a moving statement for me, as that has been my own experience. As I have come to trust in my experience more and more, I can feel exactly what is going on with every member of my staff, and I know whom I am going to see or hear from.

Nothing is hidden that shall not be revealed. The process of becoming conscious or waking up is the same as becoming more aware of what is happening. It's all happening. There are no secrets and it's all known. It's you who may or may not be aware of it.

Unless you trust in life through trusting yourself, there is no peace; there may be numbness, feeling no pain, but there is no peace, satisfaction, or real aliveness. As you trust more and more in yourself and your own guidance system, you become more tuned in to and sensitive to all of life, regardless of the form.

SIX ISSUES ABOUT TRUST

I want to help you develop the sensitivity and tools that will enable you to live your life on the basis of an ever-expanding and absolute trust in yourself, life, and a higher power. This deep and ever increasing trust will give you what you want out of life.

You were entrusted at birth with the power of being yourself. You were also given dominion over this earth, as stated in the Book of Genesis in the Bible. Out of your integrity, strength, surety, and ability, you can be relied upon and counted on. You are the responsible one in whom confidence and authority have been placed. With this being true, just imagine and realize what is possible for you to accomplish!

I want you to read this chapter in a way that is different from the one in which you may normally read. Read this chapter as if I am talking to your very heart and soul, the very core of your being. Hear me in a way that transcends your doubt, resistance, disbelief, or fears. Let this chapter resonate within you and call forth your total commitment to living from your integrity.

Life is the great experiment. I am not committed to being a success or committed to life turning out a certain way, but what I am totally committed to is the experiment of finding out where the path goes and what happens out of practicing and living by the principles of life. My commitment to the experiment has taken away my fear, for I can't fail. There is nothing to get, only the discovery of what is there. It's an incredible act of faith to trust yourself when you have little, if any, evidence to justify doing so. The spiritual life is a totally different realm from the worldly life, for the spiritual life demands that you act "as if" and skip out into the unknown. The worldly life demands that you act "when," not "as if," and that you play it safe and step back into more of the same so-called comfort, security, and the past. There is no life in the past. The life is in this moment.

You move into the unknown by being willing to trust. Trusting myself was (and is) a huge issue to deal with, as my fear of being a bad person who could make noncorrectable mistakes was activated even when seemingly small decisions needed to be made. I had a deep belief that I could hurt others and hurt myself by making a wrong decision, so decisions became "life or death" if they had to do with my work. Personal decisions didn't have much fear attached to them. I knew I'd survive. It was the business decisions, where it looked as if one failure could ruin everything, that bothered me. By living in the realm of your higher self, even the mistakes you make become lessons to insure the achievement of your goals and objectives.

When you recognize yourself as a spiritual entity, time is eternity and one form of existence becomes the next form.

There is no beginning or end. As you live from the wholeness of your life, each incident takes its place simply as what it is and doesn't become blown out of proportion. Then you find you've never made a mistake or had a failure. There is only what you did or didn't do, and that is that. There is no compromising your value or worthiness in relation to success or failure.

Death and Trust

Locked within our physiology are all the successes and failures of our biological evolution. Death at the biological level is an inevitable event in the fight for the "survival of the fittest." But survival of the fittest has no relevance in the higher levels of consciousness and awareness. Love is all, and at this level there is no competition or threat to life. Living from love is to live from ultimate trust, where everything is destined to work out magnificently for everyone. Peace and love and the joy of contribution are the prizes in the higher realm, whereas power, control, possessions, and righteousness are the desirable accomplishments (for they mean survival) in the lower levels of existence.

You experience death every moment you live. Death has always been a part of life on any physical level. Look at the huge catastrophes that have taken place on this earth; recall man's cruelty to man. There has been cannibalism, torture, and any and every type of violence and degradation you can possibly imagine. That opportunity to do harm exists within you, just as does the opportunity to be a totally loving, safe, and nurturing being who transcends time and space. Ultimate trust comes from your "commitment to the commitment"—to choose love and uphold your personal integrity, always standing for what is ethical and supportive of yourself and others. It is a matter of telling yourself, I can trust myself to do what is loving, supportive, and ethical; I can trust myself to live from my higher self and, if I don't, I can trust myself to communicate that I did not to the person or persons involved and to do what I need to correct the error.

To transcend the lower-level desire to survive at any cost to your life or the lives of others, you must realize and know that you can have what you want independent of what anyone else does or doesn't do. No one is a threat to you. Your life comes from your own awareness and willingness to have what you want and live an exquisite life.

Forgiveness and Trust

Necessary to trusting yourself is forgiveness of yourself for not being trustworthy or for being unsafe or unreliable. To be trustworthy does not mean not to be human; it means to be responsible for making amends and cleaning it up. Your word is law, and your word is your commitment of trust. That's why your signature is legally your commitment to what you sign and you are held to it. You are entrusted to yourself, and you have been given dominion over this earth, with the power to be fruitful and multiply. Your life comes out of your word. To trust yourself requires that you restore yourself to yourself by being responsible for any lack of integrity on your part and for what you can choose for your life. Your word creates your world and goes forth and reproduces itself.

To look at trust you need to be aware of decisions you

may have made about not being trustworthy or not being able to use good judgment or be counted on. You may want to look at the flip side—the decisions that you've made about the trustworthiness, judgment, and accountability of others.

As you recall times in your life when you decided you weren't trustworthy, write them down. It's common for parents and other adults to tell kids that they are stupid, irresponsible, can't be trusted, don't have the sense they were born with, don't have a brain in their heads, don't do anything right, are a disappointment, don't think, etc., and all of us have at some point suffered some of this negative commentary.

* *Examine and put in writing the occasions when others weren't happy with your decisions or told you how self-centered you were for doing what you wanted.*

* *Examine all the failures that you have made significant. If those so-called failures mean something more than what a failure is, then you allow it to undermine yourself and cause yourself to doubt your judgment, ability, and, most importantly, yourself.*

* *Recall any times when you felt you disappointed others or when your judgment or behavior may have harmed another or caused another to fail.*

* *As you write these out, you may feel sadness, grief, anger, or some other emotion. Simply allow yourself to experience how you feel. Keep breathing, and this too shall pass.*

There is a lot of grief and sadness connected with our feeling that we cannot be trusted, which, taken further, can be interpreted to mean we are wrong and incapable. Forgiveness of ourselves and others works to release the past.

On the up side, write down all the times you were able, trustworthy, and your judgment proved to be accurate. One time I looked at my success/failure ratio and realized that my decisions were right eighty percent of the time and twenty percent of the time didn't turn out. I was surprised, because I'd been living under the illusion I was making huge mistakes that outweighed my successes. Trust is a matter of being in touch with your intuition, your senses, your wants, and your experience. The more you trust, the more you trust yourself.

Trust Your Feelings

One of the tools of trust is to trust your feelings, intuition, and experience, then observe the results. By living this way you become aware of the distinction between your inner guidance system and your self-doubt and judgment system. Using the combination of intuition, experience, and intellect, you have an unbeatable team. Using the tool of self-trust and checking the results build confidence in your natural ability to know. Some of my poor choices, especially in relationships, were the result of my ignoring what my intuition and judgment were telling me was true. My worst failures were caused by ignoring clear warning signs and thinking that I could go against my real wants or what I really felt was right. It has never worked when I've sold myself out.

You cannot operate out of deception for very long. It catches up with you, and ultimately you have to pay the price. When you trust your experience, it is the truth for you. Even if it doesn't look as if it really is working out, you have still been true to your experience—and it will eventually work out. Continue on your path of repossessing your power through your inner guidance system, and little by little you will be able to perceive the very slightest shift in yourself, others, the situations you are in, and what is wanted and needed. You *do* know; you just need to *know* you know. Others know also. It is powerful to relate to others who trust and have a keen sense of energy and knowledge of how to use their inner guidance system.

LIVING YOUR PAST WISELY

Another tool to develop trust is to look into your past and recall what you call a major failure. When did you first become aware of your inner yellow light that said, "Warning: something is amiss"? What did you do about correcting your course, or did you ignore the warning? I'm sure there were other warnings, and you may even recall that from the very beginning it didn't seem right. Pay attention to your warning signs and get back on the track. If you don't correct, you eventually either crash or burn ... or you just get by, tolerating or putting up with an intolerable situation. At some level you always know, and knowing is different from fantasizing on your fears and thus making them real.

Knowing What Is Real

How to tell the difference between what is real or made up is a challenge. For me there are two feedback systems that don't lie. They simply recreate or duplicate what is actually going on. One is my body. It doesn't lie; it always tells me the truth. The other is the world around me. Both these physical systems have no life except the life that they get from me. A body doesn't make its own decisions, and neither does a car, lamp, money, job or relationship. Life is a mirror of where you are. This feedback system will always tell you the truth about what is happening with you, and this system can totally empower you to have what you want if you are willing to use it. The lack of trust occurs within our heads. You are exactly where you want to be. If you can trust that, you can count on life to say yes to you.

THE BODY AS A GUIDE

I've gone through many, many hours and years of body awareness and body work in the form of body therapies such as Rolfing, Heller, Naiger, Shiatzu, Swedish massage, and chiropractic, as well as nutrition and exercise. What I've discovered is that when I hold myself back my shoulders hurt. When I was repressing my sexuality and denying myself pleasure, I had pains in my lower back; it was difficult to exercise and run. And my stomach tells me how I really feel. I can read what is going on with others, and when something isn't right, I immediately feel uncomfortable in my body.

Body illnesses tell tales of people holding onto resentment and anger and denying themselves unconditional love.

* *Excess fat is a call for love and protection from hurt.*

* *False appetites are another cry for wholeness and satisfaction.*

* *Excessive alcohol consumption is a desire to make life better.*

Your body talks and tells you what you want and need, if you choose to listen. If you deny your feelings, your emotions, your need for love and full self-expression, your body will cut off from its supply of the vital life force. People love to deny that they are the cause of who they are. They'd rather pretend they aren't or avoid facing the truth and dealing with it. Your world is your energy in solid form. The chair at your desk is where you put it, unless you allowed another to move it.

People come up with all kinds of reasons and excuses for why their lives are the way they are, except for why it actually is the way it is. It is the way it is because it is the way it is, and you created it *that way*. The secret is to observe your life and then you'll know where you are. Use a feedback system to perfect your senses and to be able to perceive at a level where you are in touch with your deepest self.

ASK YOURSELF THIS

Here are some questions you may want to ask yourself in order to be in touch with yourself, your wants, your needs and your truth:

* "If whatever choice I made was right, what is it that I really chose?"

* "What are my true feelings at this time?"

* "What is my ideal, if I could have it be any way at all?"

* "What is my conflict between what I want and what I think I can't be, do, or have?"

* "What is it that I am afraid of losing or of seeing happen if I trust my needs and wants?"

* "Is this what I want, or am I just wanting to get even and play out my soap opera?"

* "If I dared to tell myself the truth here, what is it?"

* "What would I be afraid of if I were happy right now, regardless of my circumstances?"

* "What would I be afraid of if I could trust myself?"

You can make up any questions that you feel would assist you in getting to the truth of your own experience.

It takes courage to trust, and for me it takes a commitment to be willing to discover the value and results of turning to my personal guidance system. If you are too afraid of losing approval and making mistakes, you will have some obstacles to overcome. To live this life fully you have to be more curious about how to function naturally than interested in holding it all together.

THE ROLE OF ERROR

To learn anything you make mistakes, and mistakes are there as feedback. Use them to assist you. It takes a lot of courage to share your truth, especially if it isn't popular, and at the same time to be willing to accept and respect someone else's truth for them. To trust is to be willing to say, "This doesn't feel right. What's really going on? What aren't you saying?" when you sense a double message.

I often don't have a clue as to what the truth is or what is happening, but I do know something is going on. All I know is that I discover what's happening by getting into it. I know the moment someone, including myself, shuts down or goes away emotionally, so I usually say, "Notice that there is a difference in you that occurred just a moment ago. What is that?" People use "nothing is the matter" to shut down and go away, but this doesn't work. At the same time you can't force anyone who doesn't want to be open with you to be so.

DENIAL IS A MANIPULATION

We are so good at denying our feelings, wants, needs, and intuition that we can fool or trick ourselves. That's why it's common for people to say they don't know how they feel, they don't know what they want, and they don't know who they are or what their talents and gifts are. They have denied their experience for so long that it looks like they don't have any. There is a lot of repressed anger in people who say they don't know. It's also a way to manipulate and control others. To deny yourself is to put your life into someone else's hands. It's to say, "I can't take care of myself, so here, you take care of me."

To say you don't care and it doesn't matter is another way to avoid hurt by not allowing yourself to want what you want and experience what you experience. People give up their dreams. They give up feeling and hide out in a false security blanket of "I don't want anything, so I can't be hurt." We turn off the judgment machine and dull the pain and blanket our feelings with food, alcohol, and drugs. In the Bible it says, "Those without vision perish."

You are the chosen, you are the one who projects life out from yourself. Not to know this is truly to deny yourself the opportunity to live fully. Use the force and allow the force to work through you by your awareness.

A Final Tool

Developing your awareness skills is a vast tool that allows you to uncover your ability to trust yourself. How do you know if you are on the right track? How do you know if it's time to leave something, or if it's just an old habit pattern being reactivated that is convincing you it is time to fight or run away? And how do you know if you truly have cleared yourself of blockages to having what you want? There are several ways I know of that will give you the feedback necessary for you to know where you are.

1. You will feel open, clear, and certain without any anger, resentment, confusion, justifications, or reasons. This is an experience of certainty, without strings, unfinished business, or attachments. You simply and clearly know. Your intended result is just hours or days away.

2. You feel fairly certain and clear, but there is some inner conflict that reflects your being at cross purposes with yourself. You know what you want but feel you don't deserve it, can't have it, or that it's not good and right to have that much. You have a set of beliefs that conflict with your expressing more life and loving it. Pinpoint those values, beliefs, and thoughts that are denying you your life, then let them go and move on.

3. You are motivated by what others are doing to you; you are justifying yourself and your actions. You are placing the cause and responsibility elsewhere than with yourself. Manifestations of this can be sickness, your life not working, talking about others in a negative way, and basically feeling victimized, all of which you deal with by attacking, defending, running from, or running to. Stop and begin where you are. Look at what you want that you are denying your-

self. Do what it takes to own your experience. No one is keeping you from having what you want. Give up self-pity and blame as a way of getting what you want. Always see the payoff and the cost. You cannot afford to deny your power.

4. You think you are complete with something and it's time to move on, but the truth is that you are leaving a mess and really just walking out. It is always okay to leave what is dangerous to you or what you don't feel able to handle, and the truth is that you are always free to do or not do whatever you wish. There are consequences, and sooner or later you will have to face them and deal with them.

Ultimately you can't run away, ignore, or hide from anything about yourself. What you don't complete or deal with responsibly and lovingly will appear again. Some things become easier to handle by leaving and withdrawing from the constant emotional input and output; this enables you to expand yourself to be larger than the problem. Just be aware, and don't fool yourself into believing you are complete when you are ignoring and running away. Warning signs are outbursts or withheld communications, as well as incompleted work, finances, and relationships.

5. See things and people as they are, not as you want them to be. Trust yourself by developing your sense of observation. Observe yourself to see whether you're operating out of your "poor me" or nice-guy routines. Or are you supporting others in being responsible by telling the truth and being responsible yourself? This does not mean giving up your innocence or your faith in people and life.

Be with trustworthy people, or at least with people who are committed to their lives and their ethics. Are you willing to "be prospered" as well as to prosper? Stop living on promises unless the other person keeps his or her promises. Stop promising if you don't keep your promises, and become more truthful about what you can be counted on to do or not do.

Without trust your life is a constant search for security in the form of outer things and outer forces. Without trust you can never move into the realm of peace, love, wealth, and mastery. You are trustworthy; life is trustworthy and gives you what you are willing to have. You are the key. You are the one who must be that which you choose to experience. You can only have what you are willing to become. You can't have what you are not. The more you feel secure in trusting yourself, the more you are able to trust that God, as life, has totally set you up to win.

Exercises

1. Recall every time you trusted yourself and it worked for you.

2. Fill in the missing part of the sentence.
   a. When I trusted myself, I_____.
   b. If I trusted myself all the time, _____.
   c. When it's something very important, I always trust
      _____.
   d. I can always trust myself to _____.

3. Do this exercise with a partner. Sit across from one another and allow ten minutes for each person to complete the exercise. Person A says to Person B, "The gift I see in you is _____." (Name the quality or gift.) Then Person B says, "Thank you, I know." Continue

making these statements, naming the qualities and gifts you see in Person B, one by one. Then switch, as Person B names gifts and qualities to Person A for ten minutes. This is a powerful exercise that allows each person to feel valued, able, and beautiful.

4. List ten fears you have about trusting yourself.

5. Write down how you use not trusting yourself as a way to avoid being responsible for your life.

6. List ten benefits you believe you get by not trusting yourself and trusting others more.

7. Do the following exercise with a partner if possible. If not, write it out on paper for ten minutes. (It's much more powerful when done with a partner, however.) Sit across from one another and say only this, A to B: "I can have what I want." B to A: "Yes, you can." Do this for ten minutes and really get into it; allow yourself to *feel* the impact of having what you want. After ten minutes, switch so that B now says, "I can have," etc.

Affirmations

Read these as often as needed. Write the one that fits you twenty times per day.

I, _____, am now willing to trust my feelings, my wants and my intuition to take care of me.

I, _____, am willing to trust myself even if I fail.

I, _____, forgive my mother (father) for not trusting me.

I, _____, forgive myself when my decisions and judgments look wrong.

The more I, _____, trust myself the more I experience
that I am trustworthy.

I, _____, am now willing to be responsible for my choices
by trusting myself.

****

Get Out of Your Own Way!

****

* 3 *

Get Off Self-Pity

You may think this chapter has little if anything to do with you! That's what I thought until I closely examined self-pity and could see how it was stopping me from having the successful reality I wanted.

Self-pity is not looked upon favorably, so naturally we don't want to be labeled with it. It's much easier and more comfortable to spot it in someone else than in ourselves. Self-pity is another way of saying "poor me": "Poor *me*, no one appreciates me; no one knows how hard I work and what I sacrifice." "Poor me, I can do things better than the ones getting the big money and the big acknowledgment; I'm a victim and everyone hurts me, walks all over me, and takes advantage of me." "Poor me, I have so many responsibilities." "Poor me, I can't get ahead." "Poor me, there is no one to love me, take care of me. I'm all alone and no one cares." "Poor me, I never have any money. They made it and I didn't."

 Self-pity is the flip side of self-importance. It's an indicator of an inner conflict between you and being, doing, and having what you want. You feel powerless to get that in any other way.

When I was nine years old, my dad gave me a spanking and sent me to bed because my grandmother had told him that I'd told a neighbor that she, my grandmother, "drank like a fish." I had not done that or even anything close to it, so there I was being hurt for something I hadn't done, feeling powerless to stop him. I crawled into bed, sobbing and comforting myself for the evil done me. I wallowed in a sick kind of self-indulgence—"Poor me, I'm so good and so right, and I've been hurt and betrayed." For me that was comfort and protection. I used it for years.

In one sense, self-pity stems from a lack of assertion, and I *don't* mean aggression. I've known hostile, aggressive, forceful, and frightening people who wallow in self-pity. The form they use is blame. Everyone and everything is to blame but themselves. What I mean by a lack of assertion, or energy, is that the person actually doesn't know how to make her or his goals *happen.* Probably this feeling of helplessness stems from childhood, for at that time we are physically less able to take care of ourselves and to get what we want.

That incident when I was nine was about my not being able to take care of myself and have what I wanted, which was for my father to believe me and to love and acknowledge me for being a "good girl." Unless spotted and eliminated, self-pity affects every part of your life.

The Forms of Self-Pity

Here are seven forms of self-pity (and you may think of more):

THE VICTIM

The victim is the hero or heroine who is a do-gooder but gets the short end of the stick. He or she is the one who stops to help someone and the person they help steals their car, or the person buys into get-rich-quick schemes and is left holding the bag and owing the money after the crook has left. The victim is the one who is fighting an uphill battle and suffers along the way, all the time asking, "Why me?" and saying, "This isn't fair."

THE MARTYR

The martyr *thinks* all the things a victim thinks but never says anything; the martyr just suffers in silence, saying, "I'm fine and nothing's wrong." The problem with martyrs is that you are supposed to figure out what's going on with them, and if you don't, you are to blame. The silent but noble sufferer has been put on a pedestal and worshipped as the perfect example of righteousness and godliness.

We've perpetuated martyrdom through our religion by honoring the silent but noble sufferers who were willing to be tortured and maligned and to deny themselves the pleasures and joys of life for our sake. Don't suffer or sacrifice for me, for in God's universe there is only abundance and the joy of living. Don't make your desire to suffer "good" by calling it "self-sacrifice." No matter what good the martyrs did, they still perpetuated the belief that to contribute to others and to serve God you must sacrifice and suffer the slings and arrows of injustice.

Martyrs are those people who grin and bear it, who sigh a lot. It's a vicious circle where no one wins. A martyr is the long-suffering parent for some. If you think, "That person is such a saint to put up with that," you are talking about a martyr. The trouble with victimhood and martyrdom is that it can make others who are happy and living as they choose think they should feel guilty for not suffering. When we award prizes and praise those who are victims and martyrs, the lie of it all is perpetuated and there is no chance for release. (Martyrs are not to be mistaken for those who give truly out of their hearts without thinking it a sacrifice.) Martyrdom denies the natural ability of the individual and perpetuates sickness. To be responsible is to win the freedom to live as a healthy person.

THE SAVIOR

A third expression of self-pity is the savior. A savior is out to save the victims, even those who aren't lost and don't want to be saved. The savior is a rescuer, and the biggest problem for him or her is the lack of appreciation from those who are saved. My tendency is to be a savior; it's a righteous and an I'm-better-and-more-able-than-you attitude. Saviors control those they are rescuing and saving, thus they can even wind up trying to destroy you. They also can instill a fear that if you don't need their helping hands and infinite wisdom, they won't be around and you'll be alone.

Everyone is able, and the best you can do is to recognize that and assist people to run their own lives successfully. What I see as contradictory in most charitable projects or welfare efforts is that there is an "able one" supposedly helping an "unable one"; there's the "helper" and the "hel-pee." We've all needed assistance, yet there are a huge number of people who are not aware of how powerful they are, especially those for whom starvation, violence, and poverty are a way of life, who are still able. When people are empowered to help themselves and then to empower others to help themselves, the world will be healed. People must be fed, clothed, housed, educated from the context of *capability* and *love*.

One time I was down and out emotionally, obviously running one of my "give me more attention" rackets. I threw myself down on the floor after I had thrown a dozen eggs across the kitchen. I lay there crying and calling, "Help me." No one did, so I got up, cleaned up the eggs, and realized I had to help myself.

If the world could be saved from ignorance, the saviors of the world wouldn't have a job. That's the idea! I stay away from people who look at me with eyes that say, "You are so powerful and great and I am so helpless; save me," because eventually, when they want their own power back, I have to fall from that pedestal. Have you ever been slaughtered by the one you did everything to help? Don't be surprised; look at Christ. He came with the message of love; you'd think everyone would have been grateful.

I don't lend people money or interfere in their marital problems. If I want to give money, I simply give it for nothing and as an expression of love. The one who can and does contribute is the able one. Everyone is able and to *know that, you* must *contribute*.

A close member of my family told me a sad story of "no money." I knew she owed some of our other relatives money. When she asked to borrow some and promised to pay it back, I said, "No, you won't. You haven't paid anyone else

back. But if you want someone to assist you in being financially responsible and creating wealth, I will do that."
I gave her some ideas and told her I'd work with her every week on her finances. She hasn't taken me up on my offer of assistance. I had more to give her than a few dollars for her immediate needs. I had a gift that would make her financially able *forever*. She only wanted to be *saved*, not *restored*. A parent who continuously does this for a child creates a mental cripple.

The savior feels he or she has to sacrifice in order for others to be better off. The savior's anger manifests itself as guilt. The anger stems out of the belief that you have to save others and that you can't have what you want because you need to see to it that everyone has it also or first. Saviors believe themselves better than others and at the same time not deserving or even as worthy as others. The underdog often deeply resents his or her role. Saviors often save victims who really don't want to be saved because they are getting value out of being victims. Of course there are people who contribute to others' lives not out of sacrifice, but out of love. These are not saviors. They help others to love and respect themselves.

THE BLAMER

Blamers are the fourth embodiment of self-pity. To blame is to justify your own helplessness by making someone or some condition outside of yourself responsible. The person who kicks the cat or kicks the chair if angry is a blamer.

Blamers strike out at others, and with good reason as far as they are concerned. They feel sorry for themselves and refuse to recognize that they are stopping themselves. When we are stopped from having what we want or forced to do what we don't want to do, we tend to feel stopped in all areas. Regardless of how strong, able, talented, or intelligent we may appear, things don't work for us—it is as if there were a force pressing against us. We deeply resent and are highly critical of others. Taken to a lower level, we are suppressive of others, stopping and forcing whenever and wherever we can.

The blamer is so clouded with self-pity that she or he often takes to drink to drown their sorrows. It hurts when you feel stopped. No wonder people try to protect themselves or comfort themselves through "poor baby" or "poor me" routines. But this process doesn't take care of you; it prevents you from everything you truly want. Life offers abundance; *it's the way you say it is*. Your word is law, so say it the way you want it. Complaining *doesn't* make everything better.

THE STRUGGLER

Struggling is another aspect of self-pity. The struggler does everything the hard way. The struggler probably doesn't moan or groan, but a struggler always makes things more difficult than they are. Strugglers work five times as hard or redo things a number of times. They get up extra early and go to bed extra late. They use statements like, "This won't be easy," "It will be an uphill battle," "It's a hard row to hoe," and "You've got to be tough and bear the weight of it." They talk about struggle not in a complaining manner but as an accepted way of life. Basically they are not complaining; they just want you to appreciate them. The "poor me" routine here is "Look how hard I work and how committed I am."

I was working out on the Nautilus machines at a local

exercise gym, and my instructor said, "Relax your face when you work out; there is no need for any other part of your body to make an effort except the specific muscles you are working on." As I relaxed my facial muscles and did the arm muscle exercises, I realized that I was afraid that if I didn't look like I was struggling or really making an effort, no one would know or appreciate how hard I was working out. I was also afraid that if it looked easy they'd ask me to do more and work harder because it was easy for me. I've used struggle as a way to keep others from making me do more or do what I don't want. I could clearly see how I've used that in every area of my life as a way to control others trying to control me.

Now I do what I choose to do. I can do as little or as much as I choose regardless of what others may think. Struggle, which is negative, is "Poor me, get off my back; can't you see how hard it is for me and how much effort I give to it all already?" On the other hand results are produced out of intentionally relaxing into it, just as I later discovered in my exercise workouts.

THE ARMCHAIR CRITIC

"I'm as good as you are, so why isn't what's happening to you that's good happening to me" is the sixth type of self-pity. It's the feeling that others are succeeding and you aren't but you could do better than they if only you had the chance. People who feel this are *silently* competitive but don't actually take on the responsibility to compete in fact. They sit back and compete with the athletes, the entertainers, the bosses at work, the government leaders—you name it. They could do a much better job, but they don't. In fact, they don't do much of anything. They use this shield to protect themselves from the hurt of rejection and loss. They believe that they never have to face rejection if they don't actually put themselves out front. They don't realize they've *already* lost, because they aren't participating and are filled with resentment. They resent the one who got the raise and the praise.

Life is a wonderful adventure and *you win by playing*. Those who indulge in self-pity and a "poor me" attitude hide in the critical feelings they have about others. They support themselves by claiming that this one out there really isn't that good and explaining how they could have done it much better. There is a deep sadness in such people, as they are usually truly talented and could enjoy participating, but the fear of failure is too great. The truth is, there is no failure, only experience in the process of living. The one who wastes life is the one who doesn't play. This is the armchair critic.

THE PRETENDER

The seventh type of self-pity is, "You don't really love me or care about me, because if you did, you would..." This comes close to the martyr role, but it's a little different. These people love the feeling of rejection and loneliness. People don't like to be around them.

This was one of mine. I had the belief that I really wasn't wanted and that others really wanted to get away from me. The truth is I was trying to get away, and I was rejecting them to hurt them. Always look at the flip side—what you think others are doing to you, you probably are trying to do to them. I did this to protect myself from some imagined future hurt, in case people left me. I could push them away by pretending they were pushing me away and then blame them, even though I was doing the rejecting all the time.

It always is you, all the time. It's true others will try "their numbers" on you, but it's up to you to handle how it will affect you, how you will respond and feel. The key is to see the imagined value in self-pity and then to see what it's truly costing you—and let it go.

Ending the Self-Pity Game

Tell others about your game. To let others know your racket is an incredible release. To call yourself on your own game can release you. Warn people and request that they not play that game with you. It's embarrassing, I know, and even terrifying to reveal yourself, to show your cards to another.

As I'm writing this, I can clearly see a racket of mine I've been playing in my relationship. It's sick and it's what I've used to nurture and take care of myself. I need to forgive myself and acknowledge myself for finding a way to protect myself from hurt. Now I see I don't need it any longer. The truth is that the protection created the hurt. There is nothing to protect myself from, and to protect myself *is to create an enemy that didn't exist*. I can see I've been running this one a lot lately. It seems to get stronger when I'm close to letting go more of my ego, and my ego is afraid of that, so it runs scared.

Go for it, or you can't know the life and joy that comes from being self-pityless.

Take the value out of the lie. To imagine or believe that self-pity has any virtue is to believe there's value in a lie, because self-pity is a lie. Besides all of that, people don't like you or even like to be around you if you play games.

They tolerate you and put up with you. They actually give you what you want to get you off their backs. But it kills the true love and fun in a relationship. If you are feeling a bit of a martyr right now, surrender to it and let the ramifications of what you've done sink in. Make amends with people—they'll forgive you if you choose to drop the racket. It may be a frightening experience to live without your companion of self-pity, but you can only live anew by starting over each moment. Right now is a new beginning. There can be a tendency to blame yourself first and then blame someone else later; that's not it. It only perpetuates the game. Let it go and choose to be responsible for love and happiness this moment. Eventually self-pity disappears.

Forget what you've been taught. We were taught by parents who were taught by their parents that life is a scary place and you'd better feel sorry for yourself. Great value was put on the so-called "rat race" (existence *isn't* one) and the human struggle (which is an illusion). Because of this, we've pampered and rewarded the underdog and the victim and bombarded the one who did it easily or the one who got through effortlessly or made it to the top. We've made the underpaid and overworked person a saint and the one who enjoys life and to whom things come easily a sinner. Even sexually we've made women the silent sufferers until recently. We've actually called those who didn't wallow in a certain amount of so-called healthy self-pity egotistical and unrealistic phonies.

Accept God's gifts. To "sacrifice for God" has been the way for billions of people. What nonsense. God doesn't need anything from you, let alone your misery. God is God because God already has it all. God doesn't need your love; you need to accept God's love. Many delude themselves that they are on a spiritual trip if they travel the long, lonely road of deprivation, whether it be depriving themselves of material things, pleasure, or more. How rude to say no to God's gifts! They don't cost anything. They are free; you just have to accept.

WHAT ELSE TO DO

What else then, if you have feelings of self-pity?

Most who indulge in self-pity do it because they enjoy it, plain and simply. They actually manipulate from being weak; they frighten others through being weak. You only do this when you haven't seen a better way to manipulate, so you stay in self-pity. Why do we manipulate? To take care of ourselves and to get what we want—love. We already have it. That's all we need to know to keep moving.

You can't attain heaven on earth or total transformation and also indulge in self-pity. They are in opposition. Your good falls apart after you get it, because you enjoy the false comfort of "poor me." You *are* fortunate, and you were born under a lucky star. Recognize when you use self-pity. Look at where it exists and even where it comes from. See the cost and choose life.

You must risk and go for love and responsibility. Let's cleanse ourselves, as if taking a shower, and rid ourselves of the need to use self-pity in any area of our lives. The truth is we are able and loving right now. What you want is yours right now! Be that way and *live from that*. The choice is always yours.

Exercises

1. List ten benefits you would receive by letting go of self-pity.

2. Observe the ways you use self-pity to control yourself and others. Tell others of your ways so they will help you let go of self-pity as a way to take care of yourself.

3. When you feel yourself moving into "poor me," overdo it, over-dramatize it. Instead of resisting or being subtle, be bold and give yourself ten minutes of exaggerated "poor me."

4. What is your "poor me" act telling you about what you aren't giving yourself? How are you not being good to you and giving yourself what you need and want? Give yourself whatever that is! ✳

5. In using self-pity, how are you failing to assert yourself ✳ and to be responsible for getting and having what you want? List some examples.

6. Observe how you feel around those who use self-pity and "poor me." Notice that others feel this way when you are into it. Let it go now.

Affirmations

(Write the thoughts that come to you as you write these affirmations in the margin until the affirmations feel real to you.)

I, _____, free myself from self-pity and live fully from aliveness.

I forgive myself for taking care of me with self-pity.

God's wisdom and intelligence direct me through my feelings and intuition.

I now let go of feeling helpless as a way to avoid being responsible and able.

I now surrender to happiness, love, and aliveness in the presence of myself and others.

* 4 *

Resolve Your Inner Conflicts: Trust Yourself

A conflict occurs when you are at odds with yourself. When you are being totally who you are—yourself—there is no conflict, only a spiritual, mental, and physical alignment. That quality of alignment allows you to manifest yourself almost instantly. Creation occurs out of intention. A problem occurs when you have two opposing intentions, producing confusion and a sense of being at cross purposes within yourself. When your intention, thoughts, feelings, words, and actions are all aligned, they function like a laser beam. You basically allow the mental and physical world to be aligned with your spiritual world, and you live at a level that places you beyond resistance. Of course, it goes without saying that your motives are pure. That is, you live by the ideals and principles that foster love, integrity, and the laws of God.

Life works for us, and it requires our aligning ourselves with life. Emerson, the American philosopher, said that we need to get our "bloated nothingness" out of the way. We need to give up the inner struggle and the battles we wage against ourselves. Pogo, the comic strip character created by Walt Kelly, put it this way: *"We have met the enemy and they is us."*

All athletes, especially those who play tennis or golf, are aware that winners are the ones who defeat themselves the least.

It may seem unrealistic and hard to accept the idea that life works effortlessly, but it does. We are the ones who add the struggle, conflict, and fear and create all the negative beliefs. It takes effort and commitment to get back into alignment with yourself. It's like an automobile that works beautifully and then, little by little, falls apart. You didn't change the oil when needed. (You forgot, didn't have the money, were busy, etc.) You hit the curb a few times getting in and out of parking spaces. Someone hit your car door with their car door, and you have scratches and dents. You live in a damp climate and don't have a garage for one reason or another and the car rusts. Combine all that with an accident or two, the paint getting old and peeling, and the inner workings failing out of little or no upkeep, and you eventually have a "heap," which used to be an automobile. It is no longer beautiful or serves you in a reliable, trustworthy manner. You can be angry with the car or you can face who caused this condition—you.

Ignorance is the sin, and the salvation is awareness and commitment. People actually believe that life beats them up, works them over, and is set up to deny them what they need and want. On the contrary, life loves you and supports you totally and completely. You need to love and support yourself as much as life does. You are a precious human treasure, and all life sings your praises and is here to bless and serve you. *You can't be given anything if you refuse to accept it.* You must stop working against yourself in any manner and allow yourself to prosper and thrive in every way. Allow this in your life, and others will be inspired and enabled to treat you the same way. We need to know that there is no value in self-flagellation. There are other ways to motivate yourself and also be loving toward others.

Conflicts are about wanting what you want and your belief that it is not all right or even possible for you to have it. Conflict indicates the fear of loss. We weren't taught to know that we can have what we want without loss. Loss doesn't exist. Loss is something we made up. It's true that it appears that you have lost people, things, opportunities, etc., but you haven't. To lose you have to agree that you've lost. And what is a loss but what we label usually as an unhappy occurrence? Every loss is a gain not recognized. In my life everything that has left me or that I have left has given me something greater.

The conflict that exists when you are at a cross purposes with yourself is brought about by the false belief and fear that you may lose something important to you if you get what you want. What works is to look at the source of the conflict, face it, then let go of the "but I can't" side of the problem.

Inner conflict begins early in our lives, probably at birth or even before. The first conflict would be, "I want to live, but it's hard." Being born is not the most pleasant experience of our lives. There are cross messages given and received at this crucial time. Look at the people you know who weren't entirely happy when their children were born. The mixed message is, "We want you and we don't want you," or "Another baby and everything costs so much! We can't afford to have this baby!" Perhaps a baby is born to a mother who feels little love from her husband or mate and turns all that need for love onto the infant, the message here being, "Live your qwn life, but I desperately need you to love me and be with me."

Mixed messages create mixed purposes. You believe that you could lose either way. What is needed is for you to put the responsibility where it belongs, to realize that *you don't hurt another by living fully*. No one loses that way.

Probably the biggest challenge is to discover how to be both totally true to yourself and loving and caring about others and their needs and wants as well. There is a way, and it takes work on your part to get there, if you are not there already.

One of my big conflicts deals with decisions about what I should do. Yes, I've said both *decision* and *should*, and both are energy-depleting words—they convey an attempt to be responsible but are actually unresponsible words. That's how I feel when I find myself in a situation where the need for a decision presents itself and I look to what I "should" do. I don't like to be left out; I'd rather be with the action and the fun than do what I feel is in line with my purpose or overall goals and objectives for that day. I like to play and have a great time with my friends. For instance, writing this book is a pleasure when I'm actually writing, but it has meant saying no to a lot of other activities.

I feel the anxiety, fear, and confusion well up inside of me, and what often happens is that I don't choose, but sit on the fence, which confuses everyone around me. They know what they want to do. I have my list of what I need to do to achieve the results I want, and I have what my heart wants to do: be with my mate, children, and friends, playing. My irresponsible act has been to feel sorry for myself and dump the responsibility to choose onto others. Then, if I don't get my job done, I can blame others for not supporting me. The truth is I want to do both, and I procrastinate in my work. Also my racket is my fear of being left out, not wanted, and left behind, so I use this situation to feel self-pity, blame, and to punish others—I irritate them, cause an upset, and get my payoff, which is to feel rejected, not wanted and abandoned. The method you use to prevent *the thing* you fear happening actually is your way of setting yourself up to prevent *the fear* from becoming real. It's the conflict between "I want to, but I can't" and the truth, which is that we can do what we want by being responsible and letting go of beliefs and behavior patterns that sabotage us.

How Conflicts Get Their Start

Here are some of the ways in which conflicts arise initially and take root. Observe them so that you can dig them up and throw them out. The more I free myself from these conflicts the more I feel happy, free, and alive, plus I get what I want in all areas of my life. The added blessing is that others around me are happier and our relationships become more secure, loving, and joyous.

THE EARLY YEARS

The first opportunity for mixed messages, which produce conflict, is our entry into this world. Spirit is always alive and mature, just as we always feel and know intuitively what's going on, regardless of age or condition. There is always that part of us that knows and knows it knows, just as there is that part of us that either doesn't know or pretends it doesn't know. I tend to favor "pretends not to know" as the way it really is.

Parent Messages

You pick up the conflicts and double messages that your parents and sisters and brothers live with. As infants we are like a vacuum in the way we learn. We are dependent, open and receptive without much of a shield to protect us from the garbage, lies, inaccuracies, etc. that we absorb. Our power of conscious selection may not be developed at this time, so we tend to negate our knowing and trust in others and the data received without much filtering.

The greatest learning period in our lives is from conception to five years of age. We are set up to be programmed rapidly at this point.

Survival Training

The desire for survival is our dominant motivation, even though love is our total desire. Survival at the physical level usually takes precedence at this time and, if not noticed and put where it belongs, can run your entire life. However, the desire to be right can cause you to sacrifice even your physical survival, along with your joy and love. Your ego would rather be right and dead than wrong and alive. Be committed to love and aliveness rather than rightness and wrongness.

Mixed messages put us at cross purposes with ourselves. To free yourself, be aware and drop conflicting beliefs and behavior in favor of principles and behavior that support you and the quality of life you want.

CHANGING IDENTITIES

The second way in which we are programmed and conditioned for inner conflict is the act of our taking on another's identity. We actually assume aspects of another person for the purpose of getting that person's love. Love in this case is confused with approval and with taking on the responsibility of someone else's life or their taking on ours. The helper and the helpee are two sides of the same coin, and they are each using one another. It is noble and satisfying to aid and assist a person to become more able, but it is ultimately destructive to both parties to believe that either is more or less powerful than the other.

Fears of Inferiority

To assume another's identity is to be confused already. There are four identities. The first one is you being you. Your responses are yours, your thoughts are yours, your life is the one you choose to live. When you are yourself, you can with care assume another's point of view, another's values, another's standards and beliefs, even though what you do is choose to be yourself. If you find something of value in a another person, you look to see if it fits you and, if so, you expand yourself to include that. If not, you don't.

People can only be themselves by clearing away anything that is not themselves. The fear in this is that you are not enough—*but you are.* "If you believe you are not enough, already you are too much" is a quote from a friend of mine, Bobby Birdsall. Believing we aren't enough and desiring to add substance to ourselves motivate us to become complex and confused rather than simple and certain. To be yourself and only yourself is the joy in life. Actually, you only truly live when you are yourself. Did you ever notice how many voices of people in your life you hear talking in your head? And who is doing that to you? You are! You allow it. In fact, you choose it. The healing begins when you see this and take responsibility for yourself, your actions, and the results in life.

The Desire to Duplicate

The second identity situation occurs when you put another person's identity on top of yours and the two identities become entangled. You've heard, "Like mother like daughter," "Like father like son," "He's a chip off the old block," etc. People who live together become each other. Dogs even become like their masters (or the masters become like their dogs). It is said that imitation is the sincerest form of flattery, but that's not true in the case of personality or identity transfer. There is a law in life that says you duplicate yourself, or rather, life duplicates you. We have a compulsion to recreate ourselves and our inner images in the outer world. And we do that. The reverse of this is true also, and that is seen in our desire to duplicate those we love or those from whom we want to get love and approval. A person can be so strong in an energy draw that unless you are certain who you are and that God is your source, you can be drawn into that person's energy and surrender your own identity. This can happen only if you want something from someone else. *The person who doesn't want anything cannot be manipulated.* If you are surrounded by people who need you and want something from you, it's because you are also playing their game, not yours. Let your end of the string go and those people will have no one else on the other end. It's that simple.

When you assume or take on another person's identity you get a conflict between being yourself and doing what you want and being that other person and doing what you think he or she would do. You take on that person's ailments and sicknesses as well as try to live the life he or she lives, to say nothing of trying to live dreams that are not your own.

I felt this conflict for the first time when I went to a marriage counselor during my first marriage and found myself caught in a triangle. On one side of the triangle was my mother and how she behaved in a man-woman relationship. The second side was my great-grandmother and the way she handled her male-female relationships. The third side was me, feeling what I needed but not trusting myself or having any clue to how marriage and my relationship could work. My role models weren't succeeding; I wasn't succeeding. I had to risk and follow my inner self, which was a new and terrifying experience. It took me years to free myself of the influence of those two powerful and important people in my life. Now I can love them, but not *be* them. I can do what I want and be responsible for the consequences of my own actions. This is my life and it is my choice how I live.

It was a great revelation for me one day to realize that I needed no adult supervision. What was so surprising is that I was forty years old when I realized it. I have to remind myself from time to time that I am one of the adults, one of the mature, responsible people on earth. *If it is to be, it is up to me*. Those "they" people don't exist, and I don't need a caretaker or someone to be around to make my choices for me. Making my own choices means being responsible for the outcome, as well as all the rest of it.

* *Look to see where you have taken on the personality,
   ailments, lifestyle, beliefs, values, and identity of
   another person, especially your mother or father.*

* *Consciously choose to let go of the decision to be them or love them by being their twin. You are not like anyone else, and you are the same being as everyone at one level.*

* *Look to see if what you want is what you want, if what you do is what you want to do, and then make sure that your choices are your choices, not someone else's.*

It's so easy to write things off by saying this-and-that runs in our family. Someone famous once said, "Families are the training ground of insanity." Families are our greatest gift, but when created out of fear or lack of love they are our greatest enemy. You can't blame anyone. No one was given a manual on the rules of life (except for the Bible, and most people don't have a clue as to what it is about).

When and if you feel inner conflict, be aware of who it is in there with you who is arguing against what you want. Who is it you are afraid of disappointing? Who is it you are allowing to be responsible for making your choices?

Adopting Attention Getters

The third identity you can take on is the identity of someone you envied who got the attention you wanted. For example, if you wanted Dad's love and Mom received it, you would try and become like Mom. This would carry over into your male relationships, where you would repress yourself and try to be like your mother. There are various mutations of this game. A woman may try to become her father and a man his mother. This, developed, would have us adopting the identities of celebrities, friends, role models, and anyone we believe is valued or receiving the attention we envy.

Adoration doesn't usually work, because there is anger

mixed in with the love affair, and what must happen for the identity-seeking person is to try and destroy the object of adoration in one way or another. When you don't get what you want one way, you go for it in another way. If your inner belief is that no one loves you, you'll never get love and affection. You have to fall in love with yourself by accepting yourself. That acceptance begins this moment, as you stop pretending and projecting.

A big key in this process is to begin to identify and discover yourself under all this debris of other persons' identities. There is a way to avoid being a self-fulfilling prophecy in action, and what it takes is for you to see what you are doing to yourself and turn around. Inner conflict comes from confusion in identity, a lack of inner integrity and trust. To be restored requires seeing what you are up to and beginning the process of assertiveness to back up your intuition and feelings. No one did it to us, *we did it to ourselves* in our search for love, approval, and attention.

"An unexamined life is not worth living," is another favorite quote of mine. Things don't just happen to you. They are produced through a producer—you. They are caused by the causer—you. They are chosen by the chooser—you. And there is a higher power that is Ultimate Cause. It operates much like the wind. You can't see it, but you can feel its presence and its power. You are the navigator of your boat, which is your life, and you can be an expert at allowing the wind to take you where you want to go. You do this by turning over control of the boat to the wind and positioning yourself in the right place at the right time. Ignorance of the power of the wind can shipwreck you, and it isn't the fault of the wind, it's *your lack of awareness*. You must remain sensitive to the flow of the current, the mood of the sea, and the direction of the wind. Anyone can be a master by working it out with commitment, passion, and persistence. Navigators must know where they are and where they want to go. God's will and your will are for you to live your vision and experience love, wealth, health, ecstasy, and celebration.

Life doesn't try to dash you on the rocks. Inner conflicts put you at cross purposes, like being in the middle of the cross currents. The way out is to ride one of the currents—the one that pulls at you most profoundly.

To dissolve the conflict may require you to be a "me first" person for a while, until you become comfortable with yourself. It requires what some may call rebellion and self-centeredness. You have to start somewhere. You have to take a stand and own yourself and know who you are.

Agreeing with Others

Another and fourth identity that can be destructive is created by others telling you whom you are like—as, for example, with twins, both of whom are told they are like the other. Perhaps you are told that you are just like Aunt May, and Aunt May is a lonely, isolated person. Because everyone tells you you are like her, you take on her identity, her attitudes, life-style, and, often, even appearance.

Who we are is a space for life to happen. Life happens within you, and living is your experience of yourself in life. Basically you are empty. You are awareness. You are a being of love who projects ideas, values, beliefs, attitudes, things, and goals outward into life. You are the nothing out of which things manifest themselves. Therefore, it is easy to assume any identity you choose. People become their things. *The more you become or assume the identity of that which is false and not you, the more confused, rigid, and stuck you become.* You are caught in a system, caught in a life-style, caught in a pattern of living which closes off the real you. The real you is certain, alive, creative, flexible, loving, happy, fun, able, intelligent. The real you can, and does, choose every moment. The real you is one with the current, the wind, and the movement of life. Life flows, as you must flow. Life is ever changing and offers an infinite variety of opportunities to experience, which are made available to you.

THE INFLUENCE OF RELIGION

The third way in which we are conditioned for inner conflict is through religion.

Religion is famous for teaching people that poverty, suffering, sacrifice, loving others above yourself, and denial are what God rewards later. I don't know when this started, but to me it is a total misunderstanding of God's love and law. Making spiritual "truths" beliefs and using those beliefs to control or punish other people is dangerous.

This isn't it as far as I'm concerned. As I allow more of my spirituality to come forth I discover the absolute opposite. I experience more love, abundance, health, and ecstasy. I have more of what I want and feel a greater desire to live right here on this planet as the person I am, having the exact life I have and want. God is my source and loves me.

The Tragic Trap of Guilt

If you believe having what you want is spiritually wrong or it means being on an ego trip, you are in big trouble. The guilt conflict in religion is tragic. Children are programmed to believe they can lose God's love or Jesus' love and go to an eternal hell. Children who believe that they are rewarded for denial are being controlled by people who don't know that they themselves are responsible for their own lives and can have what they want.

The truth is that when you experience full acceptance

and love, you can and do forget about your needs and love others. Until you do, this is impossible. Life works by practicing the principles of life, and these principles are taught in the Bible. It isn't that God will love you and reward you if you practice the principles and that He will reject you and punish you if you don't. "Seek ye the Kingdom of God; and all these things shall be added unto you" (Luke 12:31) means to love God and seek God's love and grace beyond all else and then all else shall be added, or given to you.

Here is what the conflict is about: Is it okay to have what I want—to experience physical pleasure, to be prosperous, to enjoy life, to love people, to have the life I want, not to feel guilty, to have fun and be light? You fill in what you deeply desire and of course it's right. You couldn't desire it if God didn't give you the ability both to want and have it.

What That Guilt Is About

The problem with having what you want is that people who do not know the principles of life sell their souls to get it, take it from others, commit evil acts, steal, murder, rape, and pillage—and more. What you give out, you get back, always. Have pure intentions, clean up your mistakes and errors when you make them, love and empower others to have what they want also, forgive yourself and others when needed, give the glory to God, and stay out there on the leading edge of life choosing and being responsible.

Cross purposes put you in a holding pattern. You can't go forward or backward. In trying to you soon run out of gas. You must be you and live your vision! Life is for living, actualizing the self, loving and being all God created you to be. You can't do that by being shut down and opposing yourself at every turn. It takes an act of courage to step out into the unknown and risk the loss of what you fear losing the most. You have no choice. It's always life or death. *Not to live fully is suicide in small doses*. Life demands that you live and to live is to be yourself, being all you can be.

The fear of failure can arise from past failed purposes or imagined losses and will keep you at cross purposes. "I want to, but I might fail" is another aspect of, "I want to, but I can't." Acknowledge your fear, see it for what it is or once was that's now over, learn the lesson, correct the error, and choose again. *Move on!*

Ending Conflicts Forever

The challenge is to continue to open up to more love as you let down the walls and armor used to protect you. There is no need for protection, for there is no attack. To defend is to prepare for attack. There is the opportunity at every turn to become more armored, more separate from others, and more closed off from your feelings and deepest needs and wants. The deepest inner need is to be loved and accepted. Some make the decision to close off and protect themselves by avoiding intimacy in order to avoid conflict. You can have it all—the intimacy, the gentleness, the caring and love, and the being, doing, and having what you want. Why? Because you say you can. It is all yours and you have to claim it. All it takes is your willingness.

IDEALS AND PRINCIPLES

What is required to be conflict-free is to discover the ideals, ethics, and principles by which to live your life. Without a clear definition of your ideals and principles, you have no foundation. You take on others' ideals, or, worse yet, you take on their values and standards, which may have nothing to do with high ideals and everything to do with fear, scarcity, lack, and limitation. The realization of your ideals and principles will give you a place to start from and return to. You probably will not always live up to those ideals in the beginning. They are there to assist you in living the life you choose, not to make you feel like a failure if and when you stray from them. You may change those ideals and principles as you discover more about what truly inspires and empowers you to live your vision.

The realization of your ideals will assist you in letting go of guilt, for you are able to correct yourself when in error rather than play the game of irresponsibility through the perpetration of guilt, self-pity, and anger. Make certain as you choose, or rather discover, your ideals and principles that they are not selected out of righteousness, impossible standards, or beliefs in "shoulds," "ought to's," and "have to's."

If you don't already know yours, I'll give you some examples of ideals to which you might want to aspire:

* To be a living example of the Christ-consciousness of love

* To be a master of manifestation

* To be committed to serving God and His heaven on earth

* To be committed to the spiritual, mental, and physical transformation of people's lives and of the quality of life on earth

* To live in the now and experience God's pleasure as natural

* To be true to my integrity and my experience

* To be committed to my spiritual growth and moving to higher levels of awareness

* To love my husband and be committed to his living his vision and having our marriage inspire others

Your principles define how you will achieve your ideals. Here are some examples of principles:

* To handle my finances responsibly with integrity

* To tell the truth as soon as I realize it

* To clean up any mess I make; to be true to my ideals

* To choose but not decide

* To choose love, not fear

* To practice God's law as taught by Jesus

* To be open to the truth wherever I find it

* To be true to myself

* To be compassionate without sympathy, pity, or guilt

* To be committed to commitment

* To let go of what doesn't work

* To take expert care of my body

These are a few suggestions and a starting point. Whenever you feel the inner conflict that arises out of being at cross purposes, tell the truth about the conflict to yourself and choose life.

Exercises

1. Observe the dialogue between your heart and your head, and write down what both are saying. Follow your heart and use your head to assist you in having what your heart wants.

2. Fill in the following sentence. Do this with each conflict. I want to _____, but _____. Open up to what you want.

3. Consider a specific conflict that you are presently experiencing. If you could change it, how would you do so? What is keeping you from having it that way?

4. Who are you being loyal to denying yourself the life you want? Who are you afraid of losing or being neglected by?

5. List ten ways that you hold yourself back by using inner conflicts.
   a. How do you control others by holding yourself back?
   b. What has it cost you to be at war with yourself?

6. Commit to living as you choose. What does your heart tell you that you want?

Affirmations

It's all right for me, _____, to choose what's important to me.

I release myself from the need to deny myself what I want in order to win approval.

I, _____, let go of the battle within me now and side with myself.

I, _____, can trust myself to do what's best for myself and others by following my heart.

My inner wisdom is guiding me now.

* 5 *

Tell the Truth—
Your Life
and Health
Depend on It

Telling the truth will set you free of whatever ails you, but it isn't always easy. The truth is not always welcomed, yet when told as an act of personal responsibility, it always produces more love, energy, health, and power. Besides these benefits telling the truth allows you to produce what you want faster and easier. Not telling the truth produces sickness, helplessness, and fear. Telling the truth in a way that produces positive results for everyone requires skill. It means always being true to your own experience and yet remaining open and receptive to the ideas and experience of others.

We've all had the experience of telling someone our truth and having them burst into tears, or withdraw their love from us. With enough of this early on, lying becomes the safe thing for any "smart" person to do. The problem is that with lies, life dies. Lies actually do the very opposite of what we think they do.

You may be thinking, This doesn't apply to me, I never lie, I always tell the truth! What I mean by telling a lie is to alter your truth, withhold your communication, deny that you are responsible, pretend you didn't create what you have, say yes when it's no, deny how you feel, not be true to yourself, and/or say you don't know what you want or that it doesn't matter.

To have more in a have-not world involves a process of getting in touch with yourself and being true to what you discover and experience. Telling the truth, no matter how difficult it seems, has been and continues to be the single most important tool of love, health, and joy in my life.

When you try to produce results through a lie, you struggle. A conflict within you naturally produces conflict in your life. *True* prayer produces miracles, for in awareness you transcend what seem like difficulties and speak the truth. Self-expression, unencumbered by repression of any kind, allows for the flowering of the individual.

Being true to yourself is your primary responsibility. If all people were true to themselves and consistently told the truth, we would live in heaven on earth. There is a thought that people carry that says, "It's selfish to be true to yourself," and, "You can hurt others if you do what you want." That idea stems from a core belief that man is basically evil and bad, so we must control ourselves and others to repress the evil.

Man is good. It's only his thought that he is evil that produces evil. Connected to the core belief that man is evil are three other beliefs:

* That what you value is scarce

* That what you want is not okay to be, do, or have

* That you can't have what you want

Life as most people know it and live it is based on lies. Lies produce more denial, negation, and lies. The irony of all this is that the motivation behind a lie is the desire to get what one wants: love, peace, and self-expression. Having what you want is a natural by-product of being true to yourself, telling the truth, and living as you choose. The very thing we are afraid of often is exactly what we need.

Getting Over the Barriers to Telling the Truth

What is it that keeps us from telling the truth fully and freely? The fear of rejection, loss, and abandonment, which we use to deny ourselves and our power.

The truth is, you can be rejected only if you first reject yourself. You can't lose, be abandoned, or be rejected unless you reject, abandon, or desire loss for another. The fear of being attacked comes from your desire to attack. A truly innocent person cannot be harmed. We only fear what we project. We only fear telling the truth out of our fear of hearing someone else tell the truth. Your fear of hurting another is your fear of being hurt.

Some live by the sword and are conditioned to hurting and being hurt as a way of life. Their offense is their defense; just as another's defense is their offense.

What works is not playing games where attack is present. In life you get back what you put out. Put out what you want to get back, and when it becomes natural for you to be loved and give out love, love will be all that comes back.

A word of warning! Your intention in being true to yourself and expressing yourself fully must come from a desire motivated by love and compassion for others as well as yourself. If your desire to live your own life comes from anger (and I'm sure it will at first), others will feel that your anger is directed at them, and they will become protective, defensive, guilty, and angry in return. To quickly restore yourself to power you may need to do a lot of expressing, yelling, beating on pillows, and crying. Damaged people need to get angry, and angry people need to express and give up their anger in favor of personal responsibility.

For me, living is a continual experience of self-expression. Healthy people are not stuck emotionally. They feel what they feel, think what they think, do what they do, and are continually evolving into higher levels of awareness, creativity, and love. You limit yourself when your life is about getting and keeping people. Your life must be fluid, open, and moving. You can have a fifty-year-long relationship that is more alive and vital today than it was fifty years ago. In fact, that is its purpose. A holy relationship is one in which all parties become better off spiritually, mentally, and physically.

THE REQUIREMENT OF TRUTH TELLING

In order for you to tell the truth, you must give up giving others power over yourself. If another holds your job, finances, or love in their hands, you are living as you are to keep them in your life. God is your source; other people are not. Your wealth comes from the source of life within you, just as does your love. You have to love your own life more than you love being secure. Security is a death sentence to aliveness. When your fear of others has disappeared, you can surrender to others to inspire you.

A primary step in having the life you deeply desire is to commit to the quality of your life. My commitment is to love, to aliveness, to my relationship with my loved ones, and to the true nature and function of my God-self. I am not committed to a church, a religion, any dogma or doctrine, nor am I committed to any belief system, set of standards, or internal structure. I let my intuition and my inner self guide and direct me to what serves my purpose. The inner structure that evolves from my experiment in living is the one that best supports me.

By being out of touch with yourself and being more committed to an outmoded belief system and the structures of society than to yourself, you really do lose. This process starts with such questions as: Does this relationship support my commitment or doesn't it? Does this job, this religion, this form, this belief, this behavior support my primary commitment to love, myself, and aliveness?

Give others the same freedom. Realize that in telling the truth and being true to yourself, you must offer that opportunity to others. It is in our interaction that I discover myself and become who I am capable of being. I need your feedback. Telling the truth is *not ignoring the feelings or needs of others*. Feedback gives you an opportunity to see yourself in ways you could not without it. So many who are committed to their spiritual and awareness process assault others with their truth and ignore the feelings, needs, and wants of others. Listening beyond words and deeds gives you true insight into yourself and others.

DISCOVERY

Another essential step in the journey to the truth is to discover just what the truth is and isn't. To "feel what you feel" is where it begins. Women are generally more in touch with their feelings than men. Intuition is a feminine aspect of feelings. Assertiveness and action are masculine aspects. A whole person has allowed for the marriage within him- or herself of both the male and female energies. Out of this marriage spring passion, ecstasy, aliveness, creativity, peace, certainty, and love beyond expectations.

People looking for themselves often pair up with others who possess the traits they believe themselves to be lacking. A woman who believes her male side to be bad, aggressive, harsh, and evil will attract a male who believes his feminine self is weak, helpless, and something to be put down and trampled, thus he must treat this woman the way he treats his own femininity. We treat others as we treat ourselves.

That which you negate within yourself you negate in others, and that which you admire and respect in yourself you admire and respect in others. Others mirror you and your relationship with yourself.

DO NOT DENY YOUR FEELINGS

Here is a simple exercise. Feel what you feel. Be authentic. If you feel sad, cry. If you feel happy, laugh. If you feel tired, rest. If you feel angry, yell. If you feel hungry, eat. If you feel excited, be excited. If you feel doubtful, express your doubt.

To deny your feelings is to keep yourself stuck in an emotional state of depression and lack of energy. When you feel you aren't alive, dig out and experience the feelings you have been denying. Allow those feelings to surface and to be expressed.

The Two Parts of Feeling

There are two parts to your feelings: the feelings themselves and the way you express those feelings. It is always appropriate for you to feel what you feel, but it may or may not be appropriate for you to express that feeling in the way you are tempted to. You need to express your anger and fear feelings in a way that is safe for you and others. To hurt another or yourself is never appropriate. If your feelings need to be expressed as outrage, yelling, hitting, etc., you may need the assistance of a therapist. As a form of release, you can have a tantrum for a period of five to ten minutes where those involved agree it doesn't mean anything. Scream and kick your legs and arms like scissors while lying on your bed. Roll up the car windows and let go. Write out how you feel on paper until the only thing left is laughter.

SAY WHAT YOU WANT

Say what you want, but say it in a way that does not hurt others. In speaking your truth, preface it with, "I feel," "I think," "My experience right now," etc. Own your feeling and allow the other person to feel safe and unattacked. You may not always be able to do that at first. Apologize and begin again. You are tuning into your other senses.

One of the keys to mastering life is being able to say what you want. And you tell the truth when you say what you really want. No one is stopping you or withholding what you want from you, if only you will state what it is.

* Give up settling for less or for a substitute. If money is a challenge for you, don't buy the substitute, find a way to purchase what you want over a longer period of time, or say that in one year, two years, or five years you'll have it. You have the same power as anyone else and you have to exercise that power.

* Get used to speaking out about your point of view and telling others in your family, organization, and community what you want. It may be difficult for you if you aren't used to it; it's time to begin.

* Take a turn at your local Toastmasters Club and get used to expressing yourself to an audience.

* Go past your fears by asserting your needs and wants. Your power comes from being in touch with yourself, allowing for feedback from others and your environment, and asserting yourself through your words, behaviors, and actions.

* Speak your word, if need be, first on paper, then with close safe friends, and then with others.

* Disagree with others if you need to, and at the same time allow them the freedom and dignity to express themselves.

I like to use a paper and pen to assert myself first, and then I tell others. It's easier and easier for me to tell others what I want all the time. The more effortless and joyful it becomes for me to say what I want, the more I feel safe and secure within myself and on this earth. The mastery of form through trusting in God's system allows you to move beyond forms and "things" into the realm of other realities, with more aliveness and a greater sense of awe. We are but scratching the surface of what's available to us.

THOUGHTS AND FEELINGS—NOT THE SAME

Know the difference between your thoughts and feelings. When you start accepting thoughts of scarcity, limitation, fear, and loss as true and real, you are in big trouble. What

I do with others in order to clear ourselves of accumulated thoughts that are interfering with our natural flow of aliveness and love is to sit down and say, "Is it all right if I clear myself of my thoughts? These aren't real, and they are there and bugging me." Then each of us proceeds to say all the thoughts that are bothering us while the other simply listens.

Anything is fair at this time, but the rule is for neither of us to hold onto thoughts or bring them up again to use against the other. Telling the truth to another in an atmosphere of love, support, and acceptance, without judgment, is the greatest opportunity you can give yourself or another. Problems arise when you grab onto thoughts and hold them close. The Bible tells us to put a guard up at the door of our minds and not allow anything in that we don't want.

If you choose to communicate intimately with one another, first sit down with the other person or persons involved and agree upon your ground rules. The purpose of your communication is to empower yourself and the other to tell the truth, trust yourselves, love and have what you each want. There is nothing more beautiful and empowering than being able freely to share any and every thought, as well as anything you have ever done, with others who love and accept you and only want you to win.

When you clear your mind and emotions this way, you experience inner and outer movement at the speed of light. We get stuck when we don't communicate. Life goes to the courageous. If you have no one to talk to, get into a class or a group at your church or temple, go to a support group meeting (such as AA, Overeaters Anonymous, etc.), or talk into a tape recorder and erase the tape when you are through. The more others can tell you the truth, while you simply say, "Thank you, I hear you" or "I understand," the safer you will feel in telling the truth.

Shutting one's mouth at the right time is a powerful technique. Giving others a chance is a blessing to all.

CLEAR UP THE PAST

Another step in telling the truth is to clear up the past in the present. You can't carry around the resentments, angers, hurts, regrets, and betrayals of the past and be a healthy and loving person. Energy must express itself. To deny yourself, your feelings, your wants, and your needs is to repress the life force. The life force will not be stopped, so even in your repression—which is ultimately your desire for more love of life—you must come to terms with yourself.

Methods

Use whatever method that serves you to release yourself by releasing others as well. Here are six questions that may help you to speak the truth to another. Begin by writing down the name of the person to whom you need to tell the truth; that person can be dead or alive.

* What I want to say to you is: _____. (Either write this, actually tell the person, or have a friend pretend to be the one you need to talk to.)

* What I don't want to say to you is: _____.

* What I'm afraid to tell you and I am withholding from you is: _____.

* What I forgive you for is: _____.

* What I want you to forgive me for is: _____.

* What I want you to appreciate and acknowledge me for is: _____.

You can do this exercise with anyone you need to, until you feel released.

Another exercise clears past regrets and resentments. Ask yourself:

* Whom do I resent?

* What do I resent him or her for?

* What do I regret?

* What is my payoff in holding on to these past experiences?

* What does it and has it cost me to hang on to these regrets and resentments?

* If I release them all, what could I be doing with my life?

Here is a valuable communication exercise to do with your mate, or even with a larger group broken up into couples sharing the experience. Say to your partner:

* What I'm afraid to tell you is: _____.

* What I love in you is: _____.

You can make up other exercises and questions that will allow you really to get to the heart of things and release yourself and others. Keep the love level high, and remember that the purpose is to achieve more love and aliveness.

CHOOSE WHAT YOU HAVE

The final step in telling the truth is the process of choosing what you have. We do what we do and we have what we have because that's what we have chosen to believe and accept for ourselves. Out of your awareness that the choice always has been and always will be yours, you open up your inner learning capacity to show you other alternatives and options.

Two Kinds of Thoughts

The truth is always abundant, always loving, always alive. The truth is limitless, timeless, and spaceless. Delusions always express fear, lack, and loss. Every time you decide in favor of the delusion as your way to give yourself what you want, you deny yourself the full opportunity to love, be healthy, alive, wealthy, and peaceful. When you tell the truth, you think, feel, and speak from God's love and wealth and allow the creations in your life to be testimony that the truth works. Telling the truth also involves recalling the instant when you decided to get sick, be poor, be lonely, not have what you wanted, or whatever. "I did that" or "I chose that" may be sufficient for you to let go of the lie and be restored to love and aliveness.

Your word is powerful; never doubt it for a moment. In releasing the past and in communicating, you may say a lot of things that you don't want anymore. Remember you are releasing and letting go; it is safe for you to express yourself. Be conscious of your choices. Be aware that you are a cocreator with God. Your words are your tools of self-expression. Be conscious and aware of what you are choosing to create and have in your life.

Exercises

1. Be willing to live with the question of, "What is the truth and am I telling it?" This is a *constant* question.

2. Ask yourself, Where am I unwilling or afraid to seek the truth and speak it?

3. Write down a list of areas of your life where you want to discover and communicate the truth. Write out what they are, what the truth is and what you want to say or communicate.

Affirmations

The more I tell the truth, the easier it is for me to tell the truth.

Others love to hear my truth and my truth heals.

It's safe for me to tell my truth.

I, _____, have permission to be true to myself.

I, _____, allow others the opportunity to tell their truth.

* 6 *

Give Up Guilt and Say Hello to Peace and Love

You actually can live without guilt and be a loving, responsible, caring individual. Guilt is a vicious, ugly destroyer of people's lives and serves absolutely no purpose. Guilt robs you of your vital energy and your ability to have what you want.

I hope that this chapter will be your tool to eradicate guilt from your life and replace it with the ideals and principles with which you choose to live. These ideals and principles are your foundation for life and will give you the guidelines you desire and need in order to develop and fully express yourself and your inner resources.

Guilt is a feeble attempt to get what you want. It always destroys the very essence of the life you are trying to create. Guilt is totally man-made. It is never noble or valuable, and now is the time to stop its vicious circle. The truth is that you must stop this cycle if you are to live freely and openly.

I'm not saying that by reading this chapter guilt will be gone immediately, but it will give you what you can use to reach that goal. You will find that you are affected less and less by guilt.

You may be thinking you never feel guilt. And yet you may be the one who evokes it in others, or perhaps you haven't recognized it within yourself. There are those who have so protected themselves from hurt that they constantly blame others. Their fear is that if they stop blaming, they will be blamed, and they feel unable to face that. Guilt and blame go hand in hand; both are anger in disguise.

Since you can't deal with guilt (it is fake) and blaming (it is irresponsible), you can let them both go by dealing with your anger. Anger can be so frightening and unacceptable to people that many even deny their own anger and cover it up with an act of being loving and peaceful. Nothing in this book is about pretense and looking good. *Who cares about pretense? This is your life!*

To live as you were created to live requires the kind of commitment to your life to the point where only the truth is acceptable. Your health, true happiness, and inner peace depend upon your willingness to dig deep within you, even if that may be uncomfortable or painful. That lack of comfort and pain is only temporary, and the denial and avoidance of it creates a suffering, the price of which is everything of true value in your life. I'm being emphatic about this because it is so important to me and such an important key to unlocking the innermost you.

People who think they've arrived and have nothing more to discover cut themselves off from the infinite, ever growing, expanding life force within them. Life is not a destination. It has no arrival point or "I made it" place. It is a journey of experience. That is the danger of believing in success and failure; they of themselves have no value. Success and failure are merely record-keeping statements for "I said I was going to do this and I did" or "I said I was going to do this and I didn't." We place all kinds of value judgments on reaching a target or not reaching it, when all it is is just what it is and nothing more. *People are valuable and worthwhile simply because they are, not because of the goals and targets they reach or don't reach.*

What I'm saying is be open with me. What I'm picturing as I write this are the people I've ministered to who, when confronted with the need to look within themselves, avoided looking and pretended what they saw had nothing to do with them. The point I'm making is that if you are to move into the transformed life and tap into your infinite potential, you must always see yourself as *the cause* of your life and your experience. As an example: You feel guilty for something. Instead of blaming that "something" for your experience, look within yourself for the cause. Life is truly a mirror. To deny this is to deny yourself life. Again, the price of having it all is responsibility, and the rewards are beyond your greatest expectations.

Responsibility is your entry into guiltless living. Guilt is anger you don't feel you have a right to experience, let alone express. Somewhere you are not willing to take on the responsibility for your feelings, emotions, needs, and wants. Guilt becomes the answer and the way to deny that responsibility. Where does guilt come from? We learn it from others. We observe others, especially our family members, and see how they handle life. In fact, they teach us. We then try it on for ourselves and observe their response, and off we go on the guilt trail.

Our desire and need for love is so deep (it actually is all there is) that we design manipulation at a very young age to get it. We'll take attention and admiration instead of love, and what we need is to love. The turn-around point is when you know you don't need love, *you are love*. Then you are open to giving and receiving love. Love is of life and fear is of death. Guilt is a manifestation of fear and the denial of love.

The Guilt Game—How We Play

The guilt game starts early and we become masters of it. Here are some of the ways in which we play.

THE REPRESSION MANEUVER

We use guilt as a way to stifle our feelings. We learn early on to deny how we feel, as if a feeling can be wrong or inappropriate. Instead of risking the sharing of that feeling and opening ourselves for disapproval or rejection, we store it away and, worse yet, blame ourselves for feeling it. We usually get even with or punish those whom we felt prevented our self-expression. You always have a right to feel what you feel and there is a way to communicate your feelings that is clean and nonmanipulative.

THE PUNISHMENT MANEUVER

Guilt is a tool to punish others, to get even with them, to vent rage and revenge. How do you feel around people who feel so guilty about everything? They're supposed to do a job and don't and feel so guilty. How could you be upset with them when they feel so guilty and are so sorry?

Victims want you to victimize them. I may sound harsh, but my purpose in discussing this is to open us up so that we can be free to live magnificent lives. Love sometimes looks hard, but it is always love. The truth sometimes seems cruel, but *the real truth is always a release* and the most loving gift of all. The Bible says, "The truth shall set you free."

THE SELF-FLAGELLATION MANEUVER

There are those who use guilt as self-punishment or self-flagellation. Beating up oneself is self-hatred in action. You can beat yourself up physically, financially, and emotionally as well through your relationships, jobs, and whatever else you are involved in or attached to.

Self-punishment has been used as spiritual purification for years. In one's desire to be pure and spiritual, self-denial and self-punishment become the atonement for all past sins and transgressions. Such a person then has the nerve to blame God for deprivation. These people do their best to convince others to join them in their purging through punishment. Harming and punishing yourself is a sin (if you choose to believe in sin). *A loving God has never condemned you.* The truth is, we always even the score with ourselves until we let go of guilt. We live by God's grace and love.

The way to make amends is to not do something if it doesn't support your ideals and principles, and to love yourself and be good to *you*. Those who ask you to deny life and to suffer and sacrifice for God obviously don't have a very loving God. They should change gods, or at least look at when and where they decided He or She was so bad. The truth is that these people are angry but don't feel they have a right to feel that anger or express it. Self-hatred kills the joy, ecstasy, and vitality of life.

THE CONTROL MANEUVER

Guilt is an attempt to control and manipulate yourself and others. This type of guilt had been mine (even though I found myself in all the types of guilt to some degree or another). When I first realized how deeply committed I was to using guilt to control and manipulate others, I wanted to feel guilty about *that*! (Besides feeling sick to my stomach.) I decided to choose to be responsible, to let others know my racket, and then let go and get on with being responsible at a new level.

In this case you use guilt by blaming others for what doesn't work. Others feel diminished in your presence and never know when you are going to lash out at them. Others can't win in their situation, because they are never enough and what they do isn't enough or it's wrong. Your anger is based on wanting something and believing you can't have it. It's an attempt to keep from losing something, and it results in paralyzing others, or at best frustrating them as you work over them. Even if you don't say it openly, it's felt as an undercurrent. It can be a look, a word, a gesture, or some other method to communicate to the other person that he or she is guilty. It's a desire to control others, to keep their love and their loyalty. It's used to keep a mate in a marriage that doesn't work. ("How could you leave me, or do this to me?")

All this is the result of our unwillingness to be responsible for our own well-being, as well as for our success and failures. People only tolerate such a person. They are happier with others. The need to punish ourselves and feel guilty keeps us attached to a guilt generator. A healthy person wouldn't stay. When healings happen, people move on. Don't sacrifice for others. You'll only get even someday, and then they become angry, feel guilty, and get even in return. It's wonderful to free ourselves of this cycle, to step out into the sunlight of a fresh new day and a fresh new life.

THE "NO CHOICE" MANEUVER

Guilt is used as a method to make things less complicated. It is an attempt to resolve the conflict between "I want" and "I don't want" or between "I want to" and "I can't." It keeps you from having to choose and making your life simple. The problem, besides the fact it doesn't work, is that it immobilizes you or paralyzes you. Not choosing is choosing. When you want both A and B, say, "I want both," rather than winding up having neither because you are in a quandary.

To avoid being responsible we dump the responsibility on another and then blame them if it doesn't work out. If your beliefs and standards are in conflict with what you want, you'll use guilt as a way to stop you from doing that or having that which you think is wrong. You may have money beliefs that keep you inactive and stuck in a financial condition that isn't satisfactory, yet your fears won't let you get out of it. You feel too guilty to move. You must take that step out to resolve the guilt. Otherwise it becomes a downward, self-perpetuating cycle, which again can only be broken by risking in spite of your guilt.

Let me repeat, *guilt is anger that you do not think you have a right to feel*, let alone express. In this case guilt is used to keep you "good" and true to limiting beliefs and values. What you need to know is that you *are* a good person and that you can *use your conscience as your guide*, as the real test of what is appropriate or not. Look to being responsible for resolving your inner conflicts, instead of enrolling others in your self-defeating game. It always begins and ends with ourselves, even though that may be difficult to face. If we are to give up damaging ourselves and others and to restore our power to be, do, and have what we want, we must do it this way. *You can do it! Everyone can!*

THE ALOOFNESS MANEUVER

A last form of guilt is the guilt that keeps us from being loving, open, and intimate. If someone tries to get close or open up the opportunity for honest and real communication, such a person brings guilt into the space. There is no way to have a deep, loving, safe, and intimate relationship with guilt. Look at all the sallow relationships in the world and all the people deeply in need of closeness but finding only distance and aloofness. Idle chatter about trivia is the signal of a guilt-ridden relationship. There is little, if any, intensity because the hurt, anger, and pain is pushed down and an "artificial sweetener" laid over the top.

People are used to loneliness, shallowness, and scraps from the table of love and life. You must demand all from life by giving your all *to* life. Cowards don't make it and neither do plastic people. You have to be willing to get down into it, to get up and out of it. Transformation requires going back and opening all the doors you've closed and dealing with what you find in each room. Don't be afraid. *You won't find an evil person there*. You'll find a radiant, valuable, and alive human being.

The statements "Don't hurt me anymore" or "I don't want to hear about it" or "I don't want to talk about it" are clues that the fear of intimacy exists. We're afraid someone will find out about us, and the truth is *they will*. What it takes to have intimacy is the commitment to tell the truth. Be responsible for your actions, thoughts, and feelings, and desire intimacy and love more than anything else.

Ending the "Guilt Trip"

To release yourself from anything you obviously have to decide that you don't want it or that it isn't valuable to you. Guilt is not harmless, innocent, precious, or spiritual. *Guilt is vicious and nasty and deserves no sympathy or acknowledgment.* Some people actually believe it shows how concerned, loving, understanding, and caring they are, but that is just a cover for the real use of it. We have adopted guilt as a way to get what we need or hold on to what we want. But in truth, we lose by using it. We don't have to manipulate to be loved, we just have to be. Love is effortless.

It's amazing to me that we can feel guilt both when we're happy and life is great *and* when we're down and out. I see guilt as a method we use to keep us from being powerful and to keep others from being powerful, too. The truth is we don't trust ourselves with all the power and ability we have. We don't believe we can love God and also be in human relationships. We use guilt to deny our spirituality and our oneness with God.

To perpetuate this need to repress who we are we project guilt into every area of ourselves. We make suffering something to admire and acclaim. Even in advertising we tell people that if they really loved or really cared they'd buy this or that in order to be a good parent, a good wife, or good person. We have made weakness a virtue and have then tried to shame the able. This conflict generates a self-perpetuating sickness. It's time to *acknowledge the able* and assist the apparently unable *to be the able people they truly are*. What you reward increases. We must reward life working wherever we see it within ourselves and others.

Government programs that may be well-meaning at the deepest level become another form of the guilt/anger machine, breeding more resentment and disability. When you are punished for "having" and rewarded for "not having," you get cross messages. Guilt is used to diminish. Things are changing. You can notice it everywhere as more and more people are seeing the light and being restored to life. It takes committed, resourceful, and healthy people to be true to these principles and to practice them. The world is transformed through you as an example. Don't play guilt or buy into it with others.

Awareness is the key. The first act in making guilt disappear is to be aware of whether and how and when you use it and whom you use it on and for what purpose. You may want to keep a pad and pen with you, and when you notice yourself participating in guilt, write down with whom you are, what triggered it, what you did, what you hoped to gain, and what you are avoiding. Blow the whistle on yourself and even go so far as to tell the person involved what you are doing. This is the true test, because when you let others know about you and what you are up to, they'll support you in letting guilt go and in choosing to be responsible.

Look at the cost. The second action to take is to observe the cost of guilt. What I've observed in those I deal with is that it costs them love, intimacy, health, happiness, pleasure, having, doing and being what they want, and most importantly, it costs them spiritual enlightenment and the Christ-consciousness they so deeply desire. You can't be in heaven with guilt, for guilt is the doorway to hell. People must choose life themselves by an act of faith and trust. The act requires you to give up the ego in favor of unconditional love.

I know it's frightening to let go of old ways of dealing with life, yet that is what is required and nothing less. You cannot be born again by living in the old life. You must choose each moment and keep choosing forever. There is no justification for producing guilt within yourself or another especially in the name of righteousness or God. Love heals and restores us to our full and natural power.

Imagine a new way. The third action to take is to imagine what your life would be like without guilt. Get used to living without it. Feel what that would be like. Envision how you would be in each of the areas of your life. Let the guilt go as you look to the anger and begin to deal with that. Ask yourself these questions:

* What am I angry about?

* What do I feel I can't have or can't say or can't do?

* What are the cross messages and cross signals I am giving myself?

* What am I avoiding by using guilt?

* Whom am I punishing or making wrong with my repressed anger?

* Whom am I being loyal to and loving by not feeling or acknowledging my anger?

* What am I afraid of if I tell the truth?

BE A "CONVERT"

You want to convert guilt to anger, for anger is an emotion you can deal with. Give yourself permission to be angry, to feel hurt, to be afraid. Even though I've said no one can hurt you without your permission, that doesn't deny the fact that you are feeling hurt. Get in touch with the hurt, the fear, the rage, whatever you feel. We shut ourselves down at moments of trauma, and some people just keep shutting down and shutting themselves off from love and intimacy, the cost of which is everything.

Stop being irresponsible. By not being happy and whole we are being irresponsible. Everyone is capable of being happy. To not be is to deny that you are responsible for yourself and the quality of your existence. Your entire life is a projection that is generated out of you and that includes all the parts of your life and your experience of life. To live as you were meant to requires having the courage to confront yourself on all levels. It means awakening yourself and staying awake and continuously living beyond your past and your patterns. You are *not* your body or your life; *you are a spiritual being who holds life within you*. That is where the good things are, the experience of living.

Break out of the trap. Guilt keeps you trapped in your mind, your past, and old learned patterns of feelings, thinking, and behaving. People are then merely objects to be manipulated. In order for you to survive you use people as dispassionately as you would use a knife and a fork to eat— except, of course, a knife and a fork don't resent you, fight back, or try to control you. They just surrender to your use. It is evil to use people, and if we don't see this, we continue to grind up ourselves and others as inanimate things, there only to serve our purpose.

Begin the experiment. Creation is natural and happens out of intention, not out of manipulation and emotional trauma. What is required is your full participation in the experiment. The experiment is this: *to live totally and completely from God's love and mastery of the principles of life and to see how far this takes you and what happens*. Who you are is an empty, meaningless space; what you are is love and awareness with the power of creation. There are principles and laws in life, and when a person commits to the practice of these laws as a tool to experience living and a life in alignment and harmony with God and God's spiritual and physical universe, that person lives life at the level of the extraordinary or what may be called heaven on earth.

Stop the cycle. The evil in people's lives (or what is called normal, ordinary, or even hell) is perpetuated and passed down from generation to generation by the guilt, judgment, blame, justification, and anger either repressed or vented on others. The vicious cycle must stop, and we can stop it by refusing to participate. Love heals all, love restores us to ourselves and to our vision. The task may seem difficult, but the rewards are infinite and beyond our highest expectation. What we have used guilt and blame to get is ours naturally and springs forth out of love and responsibility.

Exercises

1. Whom do you feel *you* failed to help? Name them.

2. Who do you feel failed to help *you*? Name them.

3. List everything you feel guilty about (include what you wouldn't want anyone to know).

4. Next to each guilt item, write down what you really are angry about, and give yourself permission to feel anger. Your feelings are always appropriate. Forgive yourself for all of it.

5. Observe and write down the ways in which you evoke guilt in others, then tell them so that they are aware of your games and will support you in giving up guilt as a tool of manipulation and domination.

6. Write down your payoffs in using guilt on others as well as yourself. Observe what guilt costs you.

7. Describe in writing what your life would be like without guilt. Imagine a guiltless life. Picture it and allow yourself to experience it.

Affirmations

It's okay for me to be angry even with people I love.

I can have what I want without guilt.

It's safe for me,_____, to give up using guilt to control myself and others.

I don't have to punish myself for having everything I want.

I can have everything I want even if others deny themselves love and life.

I don't have to hold myself back even if others do.

Others have my permission to never feel guilty in my presence.

I,_____, support myself and others living from the sweet core of God's love and peace.

****

Accept the Best!

****

* 7 *

The Taboo Against Pleasure

Pleasure is the opposite of pain. <u>Pain is resistance to love</u>, it is withholding the sweet essence of life from yourself. But pleasure isn't something you express a desire for in public if you want to be thought of as a respectable workaholic American. Actually, pleasure is surrendering into the sweet core of God's love and living your life from ecstasy. It is my hope that after reading this chapter and doing the exercises at the end of it, you will decide that it is your responsibility to experience pleasure and that through this you will find love renewed in your life and in the lives of those with whom you are in touch.

Not to indulge in pleasure is to indulge in pain and sin. ✳ The main excuse for pain and not having what you want is "I can't help it." "I can help only *this*" and "I can't help *that*," or "I'm responsible for only *this*" and "not *that*" are what keeps people stuck in powerlessness. We've just begun to tap into the power within us and, as far as I can tell from where I am, there is no limit. Since you placed any block to power there, you must be willing to remove it or have it removed one way or another. To remove blockages you have to be willing to live without them and experience your unlimited good. If you aren't excited about and willing to live from pleasure, happiness, love, full self-expression, integrity, wealth, and health, you aren't on your own side. You are dressed in full armor and enrolling as many as possible to beat you up and play the game.

For pain to exist you must actually create it and feed and nurture it. Stay with me, as we use the avenue of pain to get to pleasure. You need to look at the source of pain and the payoff it gives you to let it go. Living *from* pleasure is not living *for* pleasure or being a pleasure seeker. Pleasure doesn't exist as something you can get; it is natural, and it is released when you stop interfering with it. If your foot hurts because you are hitting it with a hammer, stop hitting it. We'll look at both the physical and emotional and open up to pleasure as the result of the life force flowing naturally through you.

It's time to open up the floodgates and let pleasure flow. The question is, how much love, pleasure, and life are you willing to have flow through you? You are the key. What you deeply desire can only happen for you by happening *as* you. You are the miracle; heaven is you. You can only have what *you* allow, and if you block it, you can pray, cry, and try all you want, and nothing will happen except more of what you really don't want.

This book is to assist you to come back to yourself and stop separating yourself from what is yours naturally. Giving up pain as real and valuable is the price you must pay for pleasure, both physically and emotionally.

Pleasure is Natural

Let's look at the taboo against pleasure in our culture. We have put pleasure off limits, made it scarce, and given it a bad name. Pleasure needs a good press agent!

Get out the hell. Pleasure is new to me just in the last few years, and each day I give myself permission to experience more love and pleasure, both in awareness and in my body. You can experience heaven in your body and on this earth. Heaven and hell are awareness kingdoms; the former is of love and the latter is of fear. *To get to heaven you have to get the hell out of your life*. Hell is of one's imagination and is a conscious choice, just as heaven is a conscious choice. Most people are unaware that *they* actually have chosen their personal struggle, drama, and hell.

To be in heaven or paradise is natural, so you don't *have* to be a pleasure seeker. Pleasure and paradise are happening for you right at this moment, though you may not be aware of it. Pleasure isn't something you will find, buy, steal, or earn. It is a natural result of surrendering to love. Safety and trust are necessary for us to let go of our defenses long enough to allow ourselves to feel pleasure. Pleasure comes from release and letting go of resistance. You can't have what you *deny* yourself even if you are surrounded by it or sitting in it. We live in a sea of love, wealth, and pleasure, and only those who surrender to it can experience it.

Just look around you. Breath is free and breath itself is life. Notice how you stop breathing when you are afraid. Most people are shallow breathers. They only allow themselves enough breath to maintain life; they withhold the wealth of breath. To flourish is to live fully; to survive is to exist and just make it. Look around and observe the level at which people live. Their lives are purely their own perception of what they have accepted as real and available. When you notice shallow breathing, breathe deeply and fully. Get into the habit of breathing fully and enjoying the gift.

Pleasure seekers are looking for the next big outer stimulus that will make them feel good. Feeling good is not something you can get; it is natural to you and therefore already yours, *so stop creating feeling bad*. All you have to do is give yourself permission to experience love and pleasure and you will.

Why do people (or more specifically you, if this is the case) deny themselves and others pleasure? Let's examine the fear of pleasure and the purpose in the taboo.

The Fear of Pleasure

Take out a piece of paper and write across the top: My barriers to allowing myself to experience physical, emotional, and spiritual pleasure are:_____.

After you write this, close your eyes and be still for a moment. Allow yourself to recall any and every fear, blockage, barrier, feeling, or thought that denies you permission to experience pleasure. Then write down at least twenty-five blockages. Identify your number one obstacle or blockage. Use this exercise to give yourself insight into yourself and the decisions and beliefs you have created and accepted as true that actually are not true. Lies block life; the truth sets you free.

GIVE UP THE FALSE

Pleasure seekers look outside of themselves and grab onto whatever will give them a high for a short period of time before the emptiness, anxiety, and pain reappear.

To be high on life naturally requires that you stop the search and look within and discover your own barriers to that much good. Here are some false thoughts and beliefs about pleasure:

* It's wrong.

* I won't care about anything else.

* I won't earn a living.

* People won't like me.

* It's bad.

* It's the work of the devil.

* I will lose control.

* God will punish me.

* What would my father say?

* I will have to give up something.

* I will have to pay for it.

* Pain follows pleasure, so I'd better not get too much.

* If I have too much, I won't get my job done.

* People will not respect me.

* Life will be too easy.

* It's wrong to experience pleasure with everyone I
  meet.

* Pleasure needs to be saved for special times and special people.

* I'm supposed to suffer.

* Life wasn't meant to be pleasurable.

* Life's a struggle.

* Anything good doesn't last.

* I don't deserve it.

* Sex is bad.

* If it's easy, I didn't earn it.

Some of these thoughts and beliefs may be yours. When you consider that everyone on this earth has their own stack of thoughts about pleasure you realize that each person is acting out their perceptions. No wonder there are war, disease, crime, poverty, misery, pollution, and loneliness. All these are manifestations of a belief in them and an unwillingness to experience peace, love, and pleasure. Ignorance of what is available to you keeps you from the higher levels of life. It's there and can only be experienced by the willing. Now do the following exercise.

* Take out your paper and pen or pencil again, and write out how you feel about withholding pleasure from yourself and others. How does it feel to deny yourself love and pleasure? If you feel angry, write that down. If you feel nothing and you don't care, write that down.

* If you are afraid to feel pleasure, write out your experience of that fear—where you feel it in your

body. Use your words on paper as a way to express your experience of the fears, beliefs, and thoughts that keep God's pleasure from you.

* If you feel like crying, cry. If you feel angry, be angry. If you feel like laughing, laugh. Feel what you feel and write out the descriptions of the experience.

Rebirthing as a Tool

When you repress your experience, you deny your experience. Shutting down never makes life better. Open up and in the opening up to your feelings and experience you will release yourself. Pleasure is trapped within walls made of unexpected experience and repressed wants and desires. Guilt is the glue that holds the wall in place. The process of letting go actually will feel as if the walls are crumbling inside of you, and you will become as vulnerable as a newborn baby.

During meditation and through the transformation process called Rebirthing, I have recalled many past life experiences, as well as my birth in this present life. I exited my mother's womb through the birth canal and immediately felt the cold, saw the bright blinding lights, and was handled roughly by a doctor who slapped me on my bottom to make me cry and take my first breath. I was in pleasure inside of my mother, and pain was my first experience in this world. I made a decision based on my experience—"It's painful to breathe and to have a body." Recently I changed that thought and decision to "It's easy and pleasurable for me to breathe and to have a body."

People are afraid that pain always follows pleasure. That's why people are saying things such as "Things are going too well, I wonder what bad thing will happen" or "I'm nervous; it's all going along too perfectly." Because we create our thoughts, we actually are setting ourselves up for pain and disaster when we think this way. Thoughts are power because you give them power. It doesn't matter whether you are aware of your beliefs or not, they manifest themselves in every part of life and experience. No wonder we don't feel safe surrendering to pleasure; our survival instincts set us up to fear for our safety and not to trust in order to avoid experiencing pain and separation.

Rebirthing is a powerful breathing technique that allows you to release the negative and damaging thoughts and decisions you've made about yourself and others and frees you to make choices in favor of love, wealth, health, happiness, and innocence.

Pleasure is pure sweetness and innocence. You cannot condemn yourself and be totally into pleasure. Pleasure is a delicate energy and all-consuming. I recall a day when I was a child of four. I was having a very good time playing when my great-grandmother, with whom I lived a good part of my early years, called me. I heard her but I didn't want to go to her and stop enjoying myself. Finally, when I did go much later, she was angry and scolded me, saying, "Shame on you for not coming when Nanny called. I could have been having a heart attack and died because you didn't come when I called." I made a decision on the spot that I couldn't have pleasure because it could deny someone else life.

* Take a look at how you deny yourself pleasure, how
you ration it, justify it, and—if you do surrender

into pleasure—how you feel guilty about it, punish yourself, or make up for it.

* *Notice how you let people know how hard you work and how little you experience fun and pleasure.*

* *Look at the excuses, if you give them, that you use to justify going on vacation, relaxing, and enjoying yourself.*

* *Be aware of how you respond to others' pleasure, especially if it's your husband, wife, lover, co-worker, or friend. A person only resents another's having what they are not giving themselves.*

I used to be upset if my former husband felt joy in the presence of another woman. I wanted him to deny himself pleasure to prove that he loved me. Our commitment was exclusive to one another, and that's how we wanted it. Now it is okay with me that he loves to enjoy himself in the presence of women. Our agreement was for a monogamous marriage. We didn't have sex with others, as sex is a spiritual as well as physical experience of God's pleasure and something sacred between us at the time.

At one time I resented it if people I loved had a good time without me. I was afraid that this meant that I wasn't special and that perhaps they didn't need me. Now I encourage the people I love to experience pleasure, joy, and good whether I'm there or not, and I also allow myself to experience more love and pleasure. Even scrubbing the sink is a blessed event. I know that may seem like an exaggeration if you haven't experienced what I'm saying. You actually do your work, communicate with people, and live your life from pleasure. I'm not saying that I always experience pleasure, but I do more than I used to, and when

I'm into pain I let go of it faster and faster. I am willing to live from pleasure now, and I surrender into that sweet core of God's love more and more. It's the most amazing process to move into what I really want in spite of fears and observe and experience my life getting better. This is it; *don't postpone your life!* I used to postpone pleasure until "a better time," or when I "deserved it" or had "earned it."

Obstacles to Pleasure

The main obstacle to pleasure is the desire to be in control. I used to use the denial of pleasure as a way to control others. I was afraid that if I experienced pleasure, especially in their presence, they'd think I didn't work hard enough and wasn't serious and responsible enough to get their support and respect. *In the process of controlling others we are controlled.* Giving that up is the key to launching your life out into full glory. If you claim that others won't let you do what you want, *you* are controlling *them* by letting *them* control *you*.

God is your unlimited source of supply; your good doesn't come from others, it comes through you. Others are possible avenues, but never *the source*. Others only mirror your own thoughts about yourself. When something is okay with you, it's okay with others. When you are unacceptable to yourself, you find others not accepting you either. You must be acceptable to yourself and be willing for people to love you.

THE MOST IMPORTANT STEP

To deny pleasure is to deny yourself what you really want. Pain and suffering are placed on God's throne and worshipped. They are false gods and graven images. Suffering and sacrifice are not the path to salvation, but actually cities in the kingdom of hell. Pain creates pain and suffering produces more of itself, just as love produces love. *Loving yourself in spite of having no evidence to support that love is one of the most important steps you can take*.

You really only are allowing God's love to take over when you permit yourself to be loved. Your harsh judgments about yourself are self-imposed. Give them up. You can trust yourself to be ethical, responsible, and decent if you love yourself.

Look at your payoff. What is your payoff in pleasure deprivation? Why would we deny ourselves something good if we didn't believe we were getting something better? If money, power, sex, possessions, approval, getting even, being right, hurting yourself or another are payoffs to you, look again. What is all of this going to bring you if ultimately not peace, love, and ecstasy? What is your payoff? What is the imagined or real value?

THAT ORIGINAL SIN

The theory of original sin evolved from the story of Adam and Eve falling out of favor with God by disobeying God and then being kicked out of paradise into a world of pain, heartache, and struggle as punishment. Until we deal with the concept that we have betrayed God, we will keep punishing ourselves. How could you betray god? You can only betray yourself, and you can give that up any moment you choose. We betray ourselves when we make ourselves God and build ourselves up at another's expense. Then the ego-self is the favored child, the only special person. We attack all potential enemies, deny ourselves and others love, and hold our position "on top" no matter what. If this describes you, give it up. It's an endless mind trip!

Original sin is the original separation of ourselves from love and all of the good available to us. No one withholds love, wealth, health, happiness, or pleasure but you, *so no one can give it to you but you*. Forgiveness is the key. Forgiveness is the key. Forgive yourself a billion times if necessary; do whatever it takes to fall into love with yourself. You heal the world by accepting and experiencing love for yourself and empowering others to accept and experience love also.

The Choice is Yours

You must choose what your life is about. *Your life is in that choice*. I have made my choice. I do at times face fears, uncomfortableness, and concerns about that choice, but each time, at every level, I am returned to the innocence of my true self and my deep need to be who I am and to love and live my vision. I can do two things: love and contribute. It is in both that pleasure and satisfaction are mine. It is in the participation and the giving away that I am restored to myself.

True pleasure is the experience of peace and love wherever you are, no matter if it's a board meeting, a Senate hearing, an intimate dinner, or a volleyball game. You feel connected with others, you feel safe, able, valuable, and acceptable. There is nothing "to get" and nothing to lose. At this point your life begins and you are free to be all you are able to be.

DON'T IGNORE PAIN

Choosing pleasure is also choosing to experience pain. Unless you are willing to face your pain and experience it, you put a lid on your pleasure. The way out is the way through. The denial of pain doesn't make it go away, it makes you less alive. Express your hurt, anger, pain, and grief. Throw a tantrum in your bedroom with the doors closed, for no reason. Yell into the pillow, even screaming out your anger, saying everything you feel. It helps to say what you need to get rid of in a safe way. You may need to find an able therapist who can guide you in this release and support you in recovery. Body work, such as Rolfing and Heller work, has over the years been of value to me, just as there are certain communication techniques and, again, the Rebirthing process, all valuable tools for releasing bottled up and repressed pain. At one time, if someone so much as raised an eyebrow at me in a disapproving fashion, I was devastated. But at this point there is very little that can cause me pain.

There are wonderful able and trained people in your community to assist you in this process. Use them. I always seek the aid of a professional that I respect and feel safe with whenever I yearn for that kind of assistance. I couldn't be where I am without the assistance of others. I am a student as well as a teacher and my life is more important than any pride or ego.

PICK A "PLEASURE TIME"

A great way to get used to pleasure is to allow more pleasure into your life every day. I used to give myself every Monday as my pleasure day. I'd stay in bed all day and relax, sleep, be lazy, read what I wanted, burn fragrant candles, take bubble baths, and have my favorite foods. How can you get from life what you are unwilling to give yourself? You can also assist a loved one to give themselves a pleasure day.

A wonderful gift of intimacy is to give yourselves a day each week as your love and pleasure day together. Don't do work, answer phone calls, or plug away at business that day. It's your day to open yourselves to deeper levels of love and sharing just for the pleasure of it. You may at this time only be able to give yourself one hour of pleasure. Start there! Make your time for meditation, peace, pleasure, and centering. Go home to that sweet core of love within you and then live from that. The sweetness spreads. My former husband and I needed to have ourselves grounded in each other's love, or we became out of kilter and disoriented at a particular point in our relationship.

The problem with most do-gooders is that they sacrifice their pleasure and joy to help others. Teach by example. Teach love by living love and live love by teaching love. Sacrifice kills people, for it goes against life. Living is for love and self-expression. The denial of your deepest self is a denial of life. To say no to life is to say yes to death. To say no to sacrifice and death is to rejoice in life. It's always your choice.

Your Divine Right

Pleasure is your divine right and the natural result of being in alignment with yourself. Practice having moments of pleasure, and those moments will increase until one day it will be a rare experience for you *not* to be living from pleasure.

Enjoy your life—enjoy every aspect, every challenge, and every opportunity. Ultimately, no one or nothing can destroy your inner peace. The greater the inner peace, the more your outer world is peaceful. We only serve what we believe in and put our faith in. It's time to blow the whistle on the lie of suffering and sacrifice as virtues. If you truly live in love and pleasure, no one can get you to wall out your integrity—to lie, steal, or degrade another human being. Being high on life is *naturally* pleasurable.

You can have what you want if in your heart you have the desire to surrender to love and pleasure with the innocence of a child.

Exercises

1. Recall and write down every major decision you've made about pleasure, including physical and sexual pleasure.

2. Recall and write down every time you were punished in a major way for having fun and pleasure.

3. Recall and write down the beliefs and thoughts you have about pleasure as it affects you and God.

4. List your blockages, fears, and personal taboos having to do with pleasure.
   a. How do you feel emotionally regarding these blockages?
   b. Why do you hang on to these beliefs? (How do you manipulate and control others through these blockages and beliefs?)
   c. Say, "I,_____, now open myself to pleasure physically, mentally, and emotionally by releasing my blockages."

5. List ten things you are afraid will happen if you surrender to pleasure and love.

6. List ten things you are afraid will happen if others close to you surrender to pleasure.

7. Write twenty ways in which you could give pleasure to yourself. (Examples: Enjoy singing, take a bubble bath.)

8. Try meditating every day for at least twenty minutes; allow yourself to let go of tension and surrender into peace and pleasure in your body and consciousness.

Affirmations

I forgive God for denying me pleasure.

I forgive_____for making me feel bad about feeling good.

The more pleasure I live from, the more peace there is on earth.

I,_____, live from God's love and pleasure.

I,_____, surrender into sexual pleasure with my mate, _____.

I allow myself to experience pleasure in my body as God's gift to me.

I now open myself to experiencing heaven on earth through feeling God's pleasure and aliveness in every cell of my beautiful body.

* 8 *

Why Be Rich When You Can Be Wealthy?

There is a big difference between *wealth* and *money*. Wealth is a condition or state of being that is natural to you, and money is a unit of exchange or an energy flow that can be a symbol of wealth, depending upon the beliefs and attitudes of the person concerned.

This chapter concerns your experiencing yourself as a wealthy person in such a way as to obtain what you want when you want it. Poverty or spiritual and emotional barrenness is manifested in not having enough and going without what you want and need. Wealth is natural; impoverishment is false and a lie.

Everywhere you look in this universe you see wealth and life producing itself abundantly and magnificently. Wealth means your having vast and infinite natural resources to supply what you want.

I like Buckminster Fuller's definition of wealth, which is:

> Wealth is, then, the already organized human capacity and know-how to employ the fixed, inanimate, planetary assets and omnicomically operative and only celestially emanating natural energy income in such a manner as to predictably cope with so many forward days of so many human lives by providing for their (1) protection, (2) comfort, and (3) nurturing, and (4) the accommodation of the on-going development by humans of their as-yet-untapped store of intellectual and asthetic faculties, while (5) continually eliminating restraints and (6) increasing the range and depth of their information accumulating experience.

His definition is not exactly mine, as I would use the word *well-being* in place of *protection*, and place more emphasis on spiritual certainty. Yet I do agree with his definition. Wealth is available resources and your access to and use of them for your physical, mental, and spiritual well-being. Wealth is sufficiency, as well as magnificence, beauty, and excellence. Wealth is always having enough, but that doesn't mean just getting by or maintaining a low level of existence. Wealth is drawing from an ever-flowing abundance of life's intelligence, love, know-how, beauty, and resources on all levels, physically as well as spiritually.

Natural wealth is infinite. It's always there to draw upon. You have but to decide to use it. You can't waste your natural wealth within you, except by not drawing upon it. The only way to waste anything is not to use it. You waste love by not loving, not by loving too much. You waste your intelligence by not using it; you even waste money when it isn't used. *Life itself is wasted by lack of use*. And what you don't use you don't have. To have it, use it. It's false security to put one's valuables away and save them for a better time.

People die having not used their good things but a few times, if even that. Someone taught them to save the best for last. Why postpone pleasure, happiness, and the joy for living for tomorrow? *Tomorrow never comes*, or if it does, you've withheld so much of yourself and held back your life so much that when you finally decide to use it you are wasted and feeble. It's so sad to see people trying to place all life's happiness in one day. It's meant to be experienced every moment for an eternity! Good doesn't run out!

The Belief in Scarcity

What you call valuable you also label as "scarce." Scarcity is a lie, not the truth, and for it to exist it must be fed. Wealth is the truth and is always there awaiting your acceptance. It is the inner realization of this that brings a deep sense of certainty, peace, and security. If you place your security in money, exterior conditions, or material things, you live in terror at a deep level, and that shows itself as anxiety, stress, unhappiness, greed, jealousy, and other related symptoms.

Your security rests in yourself at one level and with a higher power at the deepest level. Life is certain and safe to one who knows it. To one who doesn't, it is uncertain and dangerous.

To live in an unsafe, ugly, and impoverished world is not what I call living—it is surviving at the lowest level. Life is a glorious adventure, a wondrous and lovely happening. The belief that there isn't enough or that what you want is scarce lies at the heart of poverty. Poverty results in crime, starvation, hunger, loneliness, disease, war, and just about everything else that we don't want. An impoverished person can possess fame and fortune; it isn't just a condition of what we call poor and underprivileged people. The condition of poverty exists at a deep level and is manifest in each according to his or her degree of acceptance of it. The belief in "scarcity" and "not enough" can be within those who are abundantly supplied and successful, just as it is within the obviously poor. Belief in scarcity is the underlying fact that keeps people on this earth stuck in struggle and keeps the "have's" and "have-not's" in violent opposition to and fear of one another.

THE ORIGIN OF BELIEF IN SCARCITY

Where and when does a person first believe in scarcity? It's hard to answer that because, while we can say when we first became aware of something, who knows when things were actually caused the first time? Life is a collection of casual happenings, and yet there is an ultimate cause, which is you. So at some point you chose to accept that what you valued was scarce, that there wasn't enough of what you wanted. Also, if you call something "bad," even if it's wonderful, you will make it scarce and not give yourself enough, if any, of it.

In my own spiritual and emotional work I have remembered and reexperienced decisions I made in past lives as well as at the time of my birth and shortly after. These decisions affected my living and my life *until I discovered them and let them go.*

I made those decisions even though I often was unaware

of what I was doing. As children we are vulnerable, open, receptive, and willing to learn. Survival for an infant is obviously the predominant need, besides love and attention. All communication is telepathic in nature. Even if a new person doesn't know the language or is unable to talk, he or she experiences emotions and feelings and sees, hears, smells, touches, and tastes. What are words for but to express an experience and to share that which is beyond words? Words come later to share those realizations, emotions, feelings, needs, and wants.

The decisions we make are not always based on the truth, or even on what is actually so. And infants are extremely intuitive, as they are not as yet protected by all the walls and barriers that adults have learned to pull around themselves.

Many of those early decisions have to do with wealth, poverty, scarcity, and insufficiency. Children pick up the attitudes of others around them—especially their parents. This is how beliefs are passed down from generation to generation. The Bible says, "The sins of the parents are visited upon the children." Here you have the fertile soil of the child's mind; a willing, open new person wants to be loved and needs to be taken care of. Decisions and evaluations are made at a rapid rate from a position of helplessness. If not corrected, these beliefs and decisions are with us forever, actually motivating us and creating our reality through us.

Examining Decisions

To experience the certainty of wealth in all areas of your life you must discover your own patterns, beliefs, laws, thoughts, and ideas about wealth and poverty. And you must let go of those that don't support and empower you and others at the highest level of life and living.

Here are some examples of beliefs about wealth. See if any of these are yours:

* There isn't enough.

* I'm not enough.

* If I have, others won't.

* If I have too much, I'll be bad.

* If I have too much, others won't like me.

* If others have more, I'll have less.

* There isn't enough for everyone.

* There isn't enough food, time, or money.

* There isn't enough love.

* I could lose what I have.

* Wealth is evil.

* I need people to help me.

* I can't make it.

* I'm helpless.

* Others are helpless.

* I never get what I really want.

* People won't like me if I have what I want.

* I have to compete for what I want.

* I have to hold back.

* I have to deny myself for others.

* I can lose this love.

* Men leave me.

* Women leave me.

* I don't deserve to live.

* I can't be trusted.

* Women take the man I love.

* I lose the woman I love to other men.

* Life's a struggle.

* Life is hard.

Beliefs like these affect every part of your life, for they act like a foundation upon which you are living your life. These beliefs keep you stuck in patterns of behavior in relationships, finances, life-style, and self-image. They are not the truth. Life is safe even if it doesn't look like it at this moment. The more you clear away these false concepts, the more life flows through you.

The amazing realization that came to me was that all I had to do was let go of poverty and impoverished beliefs and thoughts and I would naturally be wealthy. The truth is abundant and you deserve all the good there is. Actually, nothing is even good enough for you. That's how magnificent you are.

These thoughts become ingrained in your awareness and are reinforced when situations and relationships and conditions in your life keep proving to you that your beliefs and assumptions about life are correct. Each person must break his or her own cycle and patterns. The first step always is awareness or observation. That means seeing what you are up to. Besides the decisions you make by yourself, you pick up the beliefs, assumptions, and values of the people with whom you live.

When you love someone or want their love, you are prone to adopt their qualities of personality, mental attitudes, life patterns, and even physical appearance and ailments. You become like your mother or like your father. You will even take on that which you don't like or appear not to want. The desire to be loved, approved of, and right causes all kinds of problems. First of all, you can't be yourself, and you may not even recognize yourself. History again repeats itself, and we see families duplicating themselves generation after generation.

You may be the exception, and yet I encourage you to take another look, as you may be living a life that you believe to be opposite of your close family or parents. To be the opposite is to be the same. You are now "operating over" those deeply embedded beliefs out of fear of giving in to them, and winding up just like the people you want to be opposite of. This takes effort. But you can live effortlessly and produce results. It just takes disconnecting from beliefs that are a product of decisions and evaluations that are not true.

* *The truth is always about more life.*

* *There is no scarcity in God's universe.*

* *The belief in scarcity actually causes us to hoard, hide, and build up stockpiles of money and stuff for future use, depriving us of a high quality and standard of living in the present.*

* *Each person has to have the awareness of wealth to produce it.*

I remember having about sixty silk blouses, of which I only liked and wore about ten. I thought wealth was having a lot. What I discovered was that *wealth is having exactly what I want, not having a whole bunch*. It's like having a whole bunch of boyfriends or girl friends and not having a fully committed, intimate, loving, and empowering relationship with even one of them.

I used to have an office full of knickknacks and souvenirs. My office looked like a church Christmas bazaar. (In fact, I think that's where it all came from.) My office appeared confused and crowded with things, because at that time I needed "things" around me to give me a feeling of having. One day I cleaned out my office and gave it all away. Even though all the items were special, they didn't support the quality of life I now have. To have what you want you must *clean out and let go of what no longer suits you.*

I had to separate myself from the beliefs and life-style of my parents, relatives, and sisters—not that their lives weren't for them. But their approach to life wasn't for me. You must say no to what you don't want and yes to what you do.

Heaviness of body always ran in my family. To be slender naturally without depriving myself of what I wanted to eat and enjoy required that I let go of using my weight to protect myself and be close to my family. I did not want to be excluded, and yet I needed to live my own life. Women in our family used to say things like, "I hate that woman; she's so pretty and slender." I didn't want to be hated by people I loved for being slender, and at the same time I was angry at them for holding me back from being so. No one puts you in such a position, but getting out of it requires your becoming responsible and reclaiming yourself and your life free and clear.

Beliefs about Wealth

There is a wealth of love and a wealth of living for those who have the courage to choose. Your beliefs in scarcity can be seen by looking at your attitudes about wealth, money, and having what you want.

There are two sides to wealth: wealth for yourself and wealth for others. You can't have what you are unwilling for others to have. I'm not saying you can't possess a lot of money and possessions even if you don't want others to have it. What I'm saying is that as long as it's an issue for you, you can't *truly* have it. It has *you* and you are at its mercy. Your life is then all about avoiding what you fear—poverty, loss, abandonment, and rejection—instead of about living and enjoying playing the game of life. Wealth is the attitude that allows you to play the game of life one hundred percent—all the while experiencing yourself living each moment in God's pleasure. To do this requires letting go of not "being there."

Let's look at possible beliefs and attitudes you may have about wealth. To be truly wealthy we must look to the source of poverty. Poverty can only exist out of denying wealth. Wealth is natural and is what occurs when poverty disappears as a reality in your mind. To clean it out requires that you see it and actively work to let it go. Poverty is a mental disease that actually destroys life and the experience of living.

THE "HOLINESS" OF POVERTY

Poverty and sacrifice have virtually been sanctified by the church or religion. What were meant to be lessons on the truth about not being attached to money or material things became dogma and doctrine about the evils of money, power, and things. It is true that you are lost when you trade the joy of living for the false security and power of the material world. This is the number one issue in life. Is God your source, or is this world or you your source? Where does your good come from and where is your heart?

Having a false God means that you serve money, fame, righteousness, things, worldly power, and everything besides love. All things come from the spirit, and you actually direct the flow of energy out into your life. *If you don't know this, you live in fear.* You have two fears: not being loved enough and not having enough.

"Holy" or "holier than thou"? There is one more thing that you'd sell out those fears for—your desire to be right. You will make yourself poor to prove a point. In the desire to be loved, you will demand that people love you in spite of everything, even if you don't return the favor. You will turn your back on everything you've ever wanted in order to be righteous. The result is that it costs you everything and produces aloneness. The ego works always for separation, even from God, and from love, wealth, happiness, health, self-expression, and ecstasy. To be totally alive in love requires that you actually choose to give up your righteousness.

FEAR AS A BLOCK TO FORGIVENESS

One of the major keys to wealth is forgiveness, which we'll get into later. Righteousness, resentment, and judgment stand in your way. With these blockages in your way, you actually have to struggle to produce what you want over them, and if you do you have to keep struggling in order for your house of cards not to fall in on you. Job, in the

Bible, said, "The thing I fear is upon me." Fear is false and you give it energy. Fear may also be telling you what you need to do, but you can change that from anxiety into intuition and then let intuition be your guide, instead of keeping yourself in fear and terror. Fear in any form is you scaring yourself. It's okay to do that if you want to, but each of us can make fear disappear if we choose to. The way out is the way through.

Twelve Steps to Wealth

Take some time to examine your beliefs about wealth, riches, opulence, money, and anything that to you means prosperity and abundance. There are exercises at the end of this chapter that guide you to write down your beliefs regarding poverty, rich people, spending money, God and wealth, your possessions, others' material things.

Wealth is a state of consciousness that attracts to itself that which is like it. Wealth attracts wealth and love attracts love, just as misery attracts misery. The rich get richer and the poor get poorer out of this law of attraction.

After you have listed your attitudes and beliefs about wealth and having what you want, as you do the exercises, be sure to include your parents' beliefs and attitudes about wealth and having what you want, your friends' beliefs about wealth and having what you want, your religious beliefs about wealth. Do you see any value or payoff in being limited or impoverished? Dig it out if you do.

Take some time to list your fears about having everything you want, and include whom and what you are afraid of losing. If you have been successful, people may be unloving; you may be afraid to have what you want because you fear that you then will become an unloving person.

Here are some steps and techniques to open you to being a channel of wealth in every area of your life. To be wealthy is to know that the answer and the solution are within you. To be wealthy is to know that you are dealing with an infinite source of supply of whatever you need right now. You always have more within you to draw from. You are a genius, and that creative flow of energy is within you right now, waiting for you to call it forth and demonstrate its use.

Step 1. Wealth is yours—it always has been and always will be. Accept this as true.

Step 2. Clear yourself of your blockages to wealth.

Step 3. Be willing to be wealthy, prosperous, satisfied, and fully self-expressed. Be willing to have what you want. Give up believing that poverty, sacrifice, and suffering are noble and spiritual. Love is affluent.

Step 4. Place a demand on the life force and its supply of energy by committing to the full use of your talents, abilities, skills, goals, visions, life-style, and spiritual magnificence. Set targets that are beyond you, that make you draw upon that greater intelligence and love force within you. Keep risking, stepping out there and accepting more life for yourself. Go step by step and be sure to acknowledge yourself and God. Say what you want, and know that it's yours. Use yourself in this process.

Step 5. Let go of resentment of wealthy people and of others who have what you want. Let go of any envy, jealousy, or resentment toward people you have put in your way, and bless them for the lesson and opportunity for healing. Forgive your family, your mate, yourself, ex-bosses, government, brothers and sisters, and anyone you feel angry toward. Forgive yourself if you feel you have hurt anyone or held them back or harmed them in any way. Forgive yourself for not being enough and for being too much at the same time. Forgive yourself for wanting it all and being happy where you are. The truth is you can't have what you resent in others. Spend time loving and blessing others for their good. If you want that same good, say, "That's you, me!" Observe if and how you negate other powerful, wealthy, and magnificent people and give up doing so.

Step 6. Give up all poverty ideas, statements, thoughts, words, and behavior. Be fully who you are. Give up labels such as "underprivileged," "unlucky," "poor," "helpless," and any others you can think of that reinforce lack, limitation, scarcity, and victimhood. Speak good of life, opportunities, people, etc. When you catch yourself talking life down, say, "Cancel" and change your words. Realize the power of your word. Things are so because you say they are so, because of your words and your life. It may seem unreal, but you must start sometime. Start now. Affirm wealth, prosperity, opportunities, and success.

Step 7. Expose yourself to the highest quality of life of which you are aware. Become comfortable with excellence, beauty, wealth, integrity. Be with other people who are aligned with you, who agree with the quality of life you have and want for yourself. Put yourself with people and surroundings that inspire you and uplift you. Have the finest quality of life available. If it's not there, choose it and the opportunities will be provided. Be good to yourself and others—enjoy fine music, food, restaurants, clothes, art, and people.

Step 8. Clean out closets, garage, office, home, desk, car, etc. Let go of what you no longer want and give it away. Circulate your possessions. If they aren't good enough for anyone, get rid of them. Take an active step and create a vacuum for life to fill. If you are full up with what you don't want, you can't have any more, especially what you do want. Life is a constant process of letting go and moving on to the next level of love and excellence.

Step 9. Do everything with excellence. Excellence always produces wealth; wealth does not always produce excellence. Do what you do because you love to and do it fully at the highest level of excellence you can. A wealthy person is one who enriches others. People wonder why they can't get jobs or keep them. One reason is that they are not committed to excellence. To serve another, which is to enrich another's life through your work, enriches you.

Get the job done thoroughly and with enthusiasm. Excellence is sought after; mediocrity makes great efforts even to be noticed. Excellence always rises to the top. Excellence demands all of you. Challenge yourself; don't wait to be challenged. Do more than you are paid to do and do it the best you can. The satisfaction is your reward, and you are always in demand. Wealth is your natural resource.

Step 10. Be satisfied each moment. Always accept that who you are and where you are are sufficient. To be sufficient is to be enough, which is to be wealthy. Be committed to "I am satisfied, right now." The fear of being satisfied is the fear that if you have enough right now, you won't get any more. The truth is that what you acknowledge increases. The more you appreciate yourself, the more you have. We keep ourselves motivated by feeling and believing we don't have enough, so we postpone satisfaction and live in fear of not having enough.

The greatest of all lessons is this: Be satisfied right this moment with yourself, where you are, with others, with what you have, and with life itself. At the same time, you can set goals and objectives. To be satisfied, to affirm that what you have and where you are is sufficient, is a blessing. You can surrender into God's love and be fully immersed in the moment. This is it. Enjoy! This moment is as good as it gets, and this moment is full. Experience!

Step 11. Commit your ideas, your energy, your time, talent, money, and love into life. The law of circulation is based upon the balance between outflow and inflow. To receive you must give. People who want to experience a full life but don't contribute to life won't have what they so deeply desire. Holding back and holding on do nothing but reinforce your fears. The only thing you have to contribute is yourself, and that includes forms of your self-expression. You can only be filled by continuously emptying yourself into your work, your relationships, your activities, and life itself. The more you contribute, the more there is to contribute.

Poor people believe they are not able to contribute, so they don't flow *out* and therefore their inflow is meager. No matter where you are now or how stuck you are in poverty, you must start this flow of wealth. If you are in a soup line, offer to help serve others. Only the able can contribute, because only the able know they are wealthy. Everyone is able if he or she will but claim it and do what is necessary. People actually believe they'll have more if they hold on to what they have and spend their lives conning others into giving them what they want and need. You may not receive back from where you give, but you will be contributed to as a natural result of your contribution.

Don't give to get. That doesn't work. Make a contribution of yourself and your resources that places a demand on you, and observe the results. Able people always have what they want. To be wealthy you must forever be a contributor. A great way to contribute is to share with others and to assist others in having it all also. That action will restore you. Help others to help themselves. Spread the word.

Step 12. Give the glory to the Higher Power. Whatever your religious beliefs, recognize God as the source of wealth. It is He that owns it all and channels it through you. Praise the Lord. Praise the Holy Spirit not as an act of superstition, but in order to feel where the power comes from. Be in constant contact and communication with this Love Force. Those who think *they* are it burn out, dry up, and then wonder, "Is this all there is?" As Christ said, "I of mine own self can do nothing, except the father within me, he doeth this work."

Miracles happen as a natural outcome of surrender to God and acknowledgment that it's He who does it. You are the willing channel and blessed receiver. Don't believe me? Try it! You cannot hold the blessings that will flow to you! Your creativity, love, happiness, health, wealth, talents, and successes all flow from this source. Open yourself by continuously acknowledging God's love and blessings in your life.

There may be other steps you'll discover. Right now these will get you rolling onward and upward. Every person is naturally wealthy. You need to be responsible for your life in order to be all you can be. No one can do it for you, and no one will. It takes you, and you can do it. *You generate wealth out of yourself by choosing it*. Choose the quality of your life. Be committed to it! Live it! Responsibility is the key. You are an able person, just as able as anyone else. Everyone is able. Your gift to others is to live life fully and to assist others in seeing who they are so they too can live as wealthy and able and loving people.

Exercises

1. Visualize for ten minutes each day your being a wealthy person and especially experience yourself being wealthy and able.

2. Write down the major decisions you have made about wealth and wealthy people, about spirituality and wealth.

3. List ten ways you block yourself from being, doing, and having exactly what you want (then stop doing them).

4. List twenty ways in which you can open yourself to wealth—and do them.

5. List ten ways in which you keep yourself from giving to others because you believe you don't have enough.

6. List ten fears you have that are keeping you from being wealthy, and recall when you first decided that they were true.

7. What would your parents and family members think or say if you were wealthy and living as you choose? And how would they react if you were impoverished? How has this affected you?

8. What statement are you making with your life-style?

9. List your hidden desires, wants, and dreams.

10. What are your payoffs in not having what you want? What does it cost you?

Affirmations

I surround myself with wealth.

I,_____, am a wealthy person.

Wealth is everyone's right and by accepting it, I,_____,
   allow myself to enjoy being wealthy.

* 9 *

Money, Money, and More Money

Money has rules, and when you know those rules you can play the money game and win. Wealth and money are not the same. Wealth is an *attitude*—a place to live. Money is a means of exchange, a *symbol* of wealth. Being wealthy is being whole and satisfied no matter what the conditions of your life and specifically no matter what the financial condition of your life. Wealth is being, whereas money is a thing that has form and our agreed-upon value. Money is also an illusion. It won't make you happy, bring you love, heal your insecurities, buy you people, or make you better. Money is simply money.

False Beliefs about Money

Let's start with clearing up false information and beliefs about money. Before you seek solutions, look into the attitudes you have about the subject. Financial success is available to everyone, and the first step—which is the biggest—is for each of us to become responsible for our financial condition. You can't consciously generate anything if you pretend you are not the cause.

"I am the cause of my financial condition" is a powerful statement and one that places you in charge.

Most people are overwhelmed. There is more victim-consciousness attached to money than just about anything else (with perhaps the possible exception of relationships). Money victimhood is shouted from the rooftops. Money victims are everywhere and they aren't limited to just the poor. The very rich can also be victims of the money game. Those who are money victims blame a lot. They blame those with money, they blame their kids for being a burden to them, they blame their mates for spending too much or not earning enough; they blame the government, their employers, even their astrological signs.

It's time to stop pretending. Examine where money is an issue in your life—where the lack of it holds you back, where the abundance of it is a problem, or where the fear of having it or losing it is an obstacle. Are you a money victim or are you a money generator and curator? This doesn't have to be a have-not world. Everyone can have and know how to have. You can be the inspiration by your example. Create opportunities to share your good with others in a way that recognizes their ability and value as human beings.

We have a world full of people feeling sorry for themselves and others or resentful of others. Too many believe life to be hopeless and inevitable. Feeling sorry is a meaningless gesture. It is actually evil and limiting. There is no responsibility in sympathy, pity, resentment, guilt, blame, or being sorry for anyone or anything. Compassion, nurturing, and enabling are the keys to truly helping and assisting another to be an able, responsible, productive, and valuable human being.

Stop generating poverty. Poverty is in no way virtuous, spiritual, or inevitable. There are no redeeming qualities in being impoverished. You are the generator of poverty! Give up poverty as an option or a reality. Thoughts create their own worlds. What do you want to see? What do you want to be...do...have? It's all there for you; all it takes is creating it through you, through your thoughts and your declaration. Let God's wealth flow through you into your world. You are the cause of your finances today, yesterday, and tomorrow. There is nowhere else to look.

Look at all the underprivileged who have moved out of ghettos and are contributing, prosperous, and responsible citizens. Look at all the people born with silver spoons in their mouths who have wound up down and out. People may not want to hear this, let alone accept it, as it isn't the popular behaviorist point of view, but the conditions of your life don't make you who you are—you do. The circumstances and conditions of your life don't mean anything; they are simply impersonal mirrors of your awareness at this point in time. Who you are and the quality of your life is determined by you through your willingness to cause your own happiness and satisfaction and by your loving each moment in the moment. Things will change—they always have and always will.

To have anything you have to cause it, and to truly have something you have to give it away. You only have what you can use and share; otherwise it's as if you don't have it. Having is using and giving. It's the same with money.

Four Steps to Financial Responsibility

To be responsible for the state of your finances and the money in your life, follow these steps:

Step 1. Write down your beliefs, thoughts, and fears about money. Write down what is good and bad about money. Examine how you talk about money in each of your dealings with money.

You may notice that you resist letting others know your finances. What I've discovered is that people would rather talk about sex and their most intimate experiences than about their money condition.

Step 2. To create the ideal money situation in your life, you must begin by knowing your actual financial picture. Face the truth: What is the exact condition of your finances? By writing out a financial statement listing all your assets—cash, investments, real estate, auto—and all your debts, you will arrive at an accurate picture of your actual financial state. You may be surprised that you have more assets than you realized. It may be uncomfortable for you to face this. Use your willpower to move you past your discomfort. I always breathe deeply if I am afraid or uncomfortable. It works. You take the mystery out of something when you face it, look at it, and handle it.

Step 3. Take responsibility for cleaning up any mess, if you are in one. It won't go away on its own if you ignore it. That which is incomplete or a mess keeps you from having what you want and living fully. The energy that is available to you in the present is used for the past. You actually deny yourself more life by not clearing up your past.

If you have a large mess, start cleaning it up piece by piece. Get into communication with people and organizations to whom you owe money or who owe you money. If you have things that belong to others, give them back. Make sure that all your energy is here in the present. Then you feel clean as a whistle. It may take you some time. Be patient with yourself and feel acknowledged for your willingness to be responsible.

Step 4. Create your ideal financial picture in writing. Set money goals for one month, six months, one year, two years, and five years. If you reach them faster, redo your time line. I want you to be the cause of your finances, not the victim of them. It's important that you know how to generate income in order to play the money game.

Be a goal setter. Set financial goals that are realistic, as well as outrageous. If your consciousness for extra money is at fifty dollars per week, up that to seventy-five, then one hundred, then two hundred, etc. How would you feel right now if your income was ten times what it presently is? How would your family and friends react to your prosperity? How would you take care of it, what would you do with it, etc.? The truth is, if you can handle it, you'll allow yourself to have it, if you don't feel you can or want to, you won't.

If you've been "Daddy's little girl" and suddenly you are out on your own supporting yourself and making more than Daddy, something is going to happen in that relationship. If you and your friends sit around and talk about how hard it is and then one day you change your tune and start being positive, responsible, and prosperous, that could be a shock to your friends.

The "big kill" is not it. We live in a have-not world that is made so by people not being willing to take responsibility for their lives and especially for their finances. You are a "have" person, and that requires living in another realm or world. You live out of love, wealth, and unlimited opportunities. Set financial goals that allow you to win by moving up step by step. If you are greedy and a dreamer, this may look too slow for you. Steady Eddie gets the job done. Gamblers and alcoholics are sure to want to make a big killing fast. I used to live in the world of vague hope, until I decided to be consistent and persistent, moving one step at a time. I now get to those goals and the steps I take get bigger each time.

Have your goals be real. Read your list of goals once each day and envision each as already accomplished. For each goal say something like, "I, Terry, have $20,000 in my savings account," or "I, Terry, have the $5,000 I need for my trip," or "I own my own home, in a fine neighborhood with loving neighbors," and so on. You might say, "I have a great job, with positive, fun people where I earn $500 per week and have the opportunity to earn ten times that amount." Make your goals real, but make them make you stretch. The truth is you can have what you say you can have.

A word of caution to those of you who might become discouraged if you don't get the results you want right away. Persist. If you say what you want long enough, it must come to pass. It's like living with clogged plumbing and wondering why you only have a trickle of water flowing. *You* have to clear out the blockages and then the water flows freely and abundantly.

Handling Your Present Money

Let's handle the money you have now and set you up with a system that acknowledges the ultimate source of all your inflow. Remember, money is an energy flow; it is a system of acknowledgment and empowerment.

GIVE TO GOD'S WORK

Give ten percent off the top for God's work. God is the source of life. Your life comes from this higher power. Without it you wouldn't be here, and money and having what you want wouldn't be an issue. Your life comes from and is God. You can call this power anything, but you didn't make yourself. You can't even create without the power of creation.

Tithing ten percent of your income right off the top works. Give to the organization or group where you receive your spiritual support. It allows you to transcend your fear about not having enough and plugs you into the system of prosperity. I'm not going to elaborate. You can investigate tithing on your own. I've always had an abundant supply of money since I started tithing to God's work, even before I pay bills. I also contribute money on top of the ten percent to individuals and groups that I feel are making a difference. I do not give out of sympathy, guilt, or pity. I give to whoever is accomplishing good works.

Here is the secret of contribution: the money you give does what you want it to because you will it.

* *Don't give tokens or gestures, give out of your heart.*

* *Give because it is a statement of who you are and what your life is about.*

* *Give without strings*.

* *Give because it contributes to you.*

The spirit doesn't know getting, only giving. To people who know who they are, the idea of sacrifice is a joke. Only the able can contribute, and you are able. Your contribution is a statement of your ability. The power of tithing and contribution lies in the phenomenon of giving. What you give out comes back to you increased. You prosper out of your outflow.

There is a law of circulation to life. You see it in nature and if you pay attention, you discover it in all of life. Outflow and inflow are the giving and receiving aspects of circulation. We live in a getting, "give me" world. That doesn't work and never has. To have inflow you must have outflow, and you have to start where you are and continue this forever. If you haven't experienced this yet, you will discover that the gift is in the giving. You've always wanted to give. *Look into your life as far back as you can remember and recall the time or times when you made a decision not to give, not to share, and not to contribute*. It could be that you decided your gift wasn't enough, or that others had better gifts, or that no one appreciated your contribution. Or perhaps you were laughed at and your gift denied. There is always the possibility that you believed you didn't have enough because you could see there wasn't much and when that ran out there wouldn't be any more. Many people are afraid of being foolish and irresponsible with their money and possessions. Giving and contribution for the sake of giving and contribution are not popular. Do an experiment: On a regular and systematic basis, tithe and contribute to God's work and to that which makes a difference and observe the results in your life.

BE SURE TO PAY YOURSELF

After you tithe ten percent, <u>put another ten percent away</u> <u>*for yourself.*</u> This will be for investments, vacations, gifts for yourself, and more. Acknowledge yourself and pay yourself. You may want a vacation account, a college account for your children, an investment account, a home account, or a gift account. When you allocate money for something, you create the space for it. Have your money earmarked. Money that just sits around doing nothing gets to be used for emergencies, or it gets lost or is used up in some limiting manner. You have to create the space for something, or it has no place to appear. To write this book I set aside time to write, and so I write. If I said, "I'll write when I have the time," forget it—I wouldn't have the time.

The universe forces you to contribute one way or another. To be unconscious is to waste life; to be conscious and aware is to live fully, having what you want.

NEXT, HANDLE BILLS

Pay yourself after God's work, and then pay your bills. If you have a lot of bills, do three things:

* Work out a payment schedule for each bill that you can afford.

* Find ways to increase your income.

* Keep your inflow higher than your outflow.

Be careful of buying and spending over your head. That in itself can weigh you down. You can have what you want when you live in the world of miracles and practicality. Envision your dreams coming true *while you are balancing your checkbook and gladly paying your bills*.

I write "Thank you" under my signature on my checks as a reminder that money is acknowledgment. You are not your money. Money is there to serve you. Another thing I do is to acknowledge my unlimited wealth and abundance every time I circulate money. I say something like, "This money blesses the person who receives it and blesses me and increases my prosperity." Say things like, "Money comes to me easily," "Money flows to me freely and I enjoy it," or "I am a money magnet, and I attract wealth and prosperity." Make up thoughts that say what you want to be, do, and have. Things are thoughts made solid. I never say I can't afford something. What I say is if I want that, I can have it. A lot of what you think about having you don't even want. It's an excuse to make you feel poor and unable. As for what you do want, get it and stop wishing, hoping, and whining.

Buy lunch for prosperous people. Be the one to feel able. Reverend Ike, the prosperity minister and a good friend of mine, says, "The way to help the poor is to not be one of them." If they only knew that their world is of their own making, they'd start making it work. This book won't do you any good if you argue with or question what I want to say. Do the things recommended here one hundred percent and then let's talk. This works. I know because it's worked for me. The truth is *I* work. I generate the life I want out of God's love and wealth.

Break your poverty patterns, and surrender into the love and wealth that is natural to you. You'll go through many stages of growth and each has a gift. The secret is to keep moving. Don't stop, the best is yet to come.

GIVE, DON'T SEEK TO GET

Here is a system to assist you in being aware of the talents, services, and products that you can contribute. Someone said, "One who is wealthy is one who enriches others." For me this has been true. Life gives to me what I give to life. What I hold back from life, life holds back from me. Look to see what you don't have, and you will find that it is exactly that which you are not contributing. That which you don't contribute is also that which you are unwilling to receive. So you see, it's a circle that you break out of by contributing, by giving.

The more people you enrich and serve or contribute to, the more you are acknowledged and enriched. People pay for what they consider desirable and valuable. Money serves as the trading stamps to get what you consider desirable and valuable. When you offer a service or a product that truly contributes to the quality of a person's life and empowers them to be all they can be and live their vision, money will no longer be an issue. *Money is an issue for those who are more interested in getting money than in contributing to others.* Their lack of money shows that.

By the way, you can sell drugs, steal, lie, cheat, and do all sorts of unethical things to get money, but you pay a price for this with your life. I'm talking about being ethical and highly principled as you go with the flow. It won't do you any good to just get money.

Life works effortlessly when you practice the principles of love. Life provides for you in an abundant and even opulent manner. Being true to yourself and true to your ethics and integrity allows you to flourish. To live any other way is thousands of times worse than doing nothing.

Finding Abundance Through Service

To find the valuable service and/or product you can give, start by writing down the valuable and desirable services and products you offer in your work. I'm talking about the final product or service you give to someone in exchange for money or something of value. Value is determined by the client or customer.

Set aside gifts, alimony, legal judgments, insurance, welfare, and loans. What I want you to look at is the valuable service or product that you have to offer others.

Your valuable services and products might be books, plumbing service, house cleaning, seminars, jewelry, medical care, wooden spoons, painting, needlework, gardening—anything.

After making your list of valuable services and products, write beside each one how you could improve its quality, its desirability, and its value. There is always a demand for excellence. You are enriched spiritually, mentally, and emotionally by your commitment to quality and customer service. Your services and products are statements of you.

IF YOU AREN'T SURE

If you aren't sure what valuable services you have to offer or you don't like what you are doing at the present, write a list of every job for which you've ever received money. Also write down a list of abilities, jobs, or skills you would like to master. Have some fun and create it the way you want it. In other words, what would you want to have as your valuable service and/or product?

Listen! Find what is wanted and needed and deliver that. Give up concern as to whether you will succeed or fail, and <u>look for what's wanted and needed.</u> Get your attention off yourself; reach beyond your concern as to whether you are appreciated or not, and get the job done. One who can be counted on under any and all circumstances to get the job done has the most valuable asset in the world. Combine love and getting the job done and, wow, what a duo! I used to be more committed to looking like I was getting the job done than to actually getting it done. Thinking about doing something and actually doing it are two different things— one is limiting and one is empowering.

If you persist and work smart, you will move to the top. The top is not crowded, for few have that level of commitment. The top is just a figure of speech. It is not a destination and doesn't mean anything. It's simply a statement about the quality and commitment of your service and product. <u>Move from a getting to a giving and contributing consciousnes</u>s.

PRODUCING RESULTS PRODUCES RESULTS

It is important that you be paid or compensated for the results you are producing. You are not being paid for being a good guy or because you show up and are a worthwhile human being. You are paid to produce results, to deliver a service or product. All the rest is wonderful but has nothing to do with getting paid. What are you delivering?

When you want to double or triple your income, you must go beyond the box that you normally live in. People don't usually think *for themselves*; they think the thoughts of a person with a certain set of beliefs and concepts. Don't let your life be determined by preconceived ideas and beliefs about what is important to you. Project what you want in your mind out beyond the box and out beyond your normal way of seeing, hearing, and thinking. If you think you are stuck, live in *creation* in the future, not in *reaction* to the past. Be a miracle worker, not one of the cattle herded and controlled by their ignorance. You are in charge and God is in control. Nothing is limiting you but yourself.

Expand yourself. How can you be in two or more places at one time? Leverage yourself! Find ways to offer your service and products through others who can also experience fulfillment and contribution by working with you. I can clean this one house every day and earn X number of dollars. I can also employ others whom I've trained to be at the same level of excellence so that I can have more of me out there. Now you have an organization and an opportunity for the team members to empower each other as well as the customer.

See the two worlds. What I've discovered with money is that to have it and have it be of benefit to you and others, you have to enjoy it and appreciate what it is as well as what it isn't. You have to love life and to give yourself permission to be all that you can be. There are two worlds: a world with money and a world without. The world without is the world of creation, the world of imagination, the realm of spirit, love, satisfaction, and peace. You can't use money to buy you any of that, but in the world of money you can have and enjoy the use of money.

Play the game of manifestation. As you observe yourself and money, be willing to let your presence disappear, and dissolve your current belief system and fundamental operating principles. Be willing to be the one to *cause* your finances and to *cause* your life. You don't need to worry about it or be panicked; it's all moving in an upward direction. Be wealthy. Be the one who lives from creation. Play the game of manifestation.

Nothing is sadder than an able person who could move mountains, heal the sick, and live his or her vision but doesn't know it. Almost everyone is able, and even those who truly aren't still deserve respect, dignity, and love, for they, too, have a contribution to make and a gift to give. Those who have are the ones who will turn their world around through their example, teaching, inspiring, and empowering others to own their power and to be first-class citizens. God's love and power is available to anyone who says, "Use me, I'm willing."

How to Get Where You Want to Go

For you to get where you want to go requires that you be there first. The first step is your arrival. Let me explain. The basic action of the state of being is duplication. God recreates himself or itself. Creation is a natural, spontaneous, and automatic action, the result of that basic duplication. Your life is a duplication of your self, of your awareness. The biggest block for most people is their denial of this principle.

You either duplicate your ego, fears, or nightmares or you duplicate love, wealth, and the celebration of life. The truth is you don't do anything; it is done through you. You become the fertile soil in which seeds are planted and grow into a crop. The crop is contained within the seed. The seed is complete in itself, and for it to grow into what it is, it goes through its process. The seed being planted is the action needed to bring forth the crop to harvest. Before the planting is the creation, or the recognition, of the fact "I have a crop to harvest and enjoy." You don't make the seed and you can't make it happen—it happens just because that's how it works. Whether you are growing weeds or flowers and plants that you can enjoy, you are the planter, the soil, the seed, the crop, and the consumer.

To get where you want to go places a demand on you to examine yourself, how you function, and the process of duplication and creation.

You cannot *not* be where you intended to be. In other words, where you are is where you *intended* to be. You may say, "That's ridiculous" or "How does where I am have anything to do with me?" What I want is for you to stay open with me and to look into yourself. It is within yourself that you will discover what it takes to get where you want to go.

IT'S NOT "OUT THERE"

The first place people usually begin is "out there" some-where. They look outside of themselves for their answers and then start looking for solutions or methods to change things. It's in this realm of awareness that people adopt their belief system about life. It's the how-to syndrome. When you first ask yourself "How do I get there?" you are starting in the wrong location. If you use a how-to system you believe that there is a specific way to do things, an already predetermined path to take and a set of things to do that will get you "there." Common in this realm are statements and thoughts such as:

* Why does he get to have that?

* She got that and she isn't even as good as I am.

* I'll never make it, because I don't know the right people.

* There isn't enough money for me to do that.

* I want love, so I'll have to give up success in business.

* It will never happen because I don't have the education.

* Everything I do never gets me anywhere.

These are just a few of the thoughts and beliefs that plague people who think that the answer is in the system, not in themselves. We need to look at ourselves and the way we mold our lives. Look at your attitudes, beliefs, assumptions, and thoughts about how you or anyone else can be and have what you want. The truth is you want what you want and you can't stop that—it springs up from within you. What doesn't work is to believe that you have to *do* anything other than say what you want, be committed to it, and create the context of having it already.

People's beliefs in lack and limitation become their ground of being or the soil in which they plant their seeds. If your soil is undernourished, your seeds will produce weak plants if anything at all. You can plant seeds all day and all year, and all you will grow is frustration, discouragement, and failure. Each time you plant the seeds you'll be hopeful, and each time nothing grows you will become frustrated, and so the cycle continues. After a while, people stop playing big. They give up their dreams and settle for whatever comes their way. If your consciousness or the soil of self says there is no way or you will always lose eventually, no matter what, you are stopping yourself, giving in to the fear of eventual loss. You create the door that closes and keeps you from going further.

Remember these points:

* *Life is abundant.*

* *You can always have what you want.*

* *There are always solutions.*

* *In truth, life gets better.*

There is no lack of solutions; there is no lack of how to's and no lack of opportunities. We have to allow ourselves to assume a whole new way of being and perceiving life.

The Four Corners of Truth

Allow yourself to accept as your ground of being the following truths.

TRUTH NO. 1

Abundance and wealth are natural. There is abundant supply, always enough at the highest level, and a quality existence for everyone. Whatever you want and need you already have; it is available for you. You merely have to claim it. It's yours by right of your saying it is.

TRUTH NO. 2

There is always a way and a solution. It is for everyone's highest good, with no one excluded and everyone included. Contained within every seed is everything it takes for the seed to fulfill itself, even to duplicate and produce more of itself automatically. Every idea or dream you have also has everything in it to produce itself. It requires your getting out of the way and being willing to let things work for you.

TRUTH NO. 3

The only inevitable part of life is love. You cannot stop God's plan for you; you can only resist it and delay it in your life. What is inevitable is living your vision, loving and being loved, and being secure and safe in God's love and wealth. There is no plan for your demise and downfall; you make that up.

TRUTH NO. 4

You have what it takes. It all comes out of you as a channel or vehicle of God's power. Whatever you want and need flows out from you. You have the ability to call forth into being what you say you will. You are a fountain of infinite supply and creativity, fed by an inner spring. The purpose of life is living, and living is experiencing yourself as being alive, whole, loving, and one with God. Actually, your experience of you is always valid and valuable, whatever that experience may be. To shut down on one experience because of another is not to be fully alive. It is in the full expression of the experience of living that life becomes ecstasy.

The Aspects of "Getting There"

Getting to where you want to go is actually a game. It's living that isn't a game. If you don't know the rules for life and how to get where you want to go, living isn't much fun and *can* be a nightmare. The more you strengthen your ability to play the game and win, the more living is an experience of love and joy.

YOU ARE THE GENERATOR

The first aspect of how to get where you want to go is to realize and directly experience that you are the one who makes your goal become a reality. You can only have what you give space to. You can't expect to have what you deny. It all flows out of you. You generate.

OPEN YOURSELF TO THE TRUTH

The second aspect is to examine yourself and look deeply into what it takes to get where you want to go and whether you really think you can do it. Do you feel there is a price to pay for getting there? Look into yourself and bring those thoughts out into the open and discover them. Open yourself to the truth of love and wealth and the inevitability of your being, doing, and having what you want. Be willing not to have quick solutions—just *be there*, without any answers. Write down the truth about your beliefs, fears, and thoughts. After that is complete, go to the third aspect of how to get where you want to go.

BE THERE NOW

The third aspect is for you to set a context that will allow you to manifest your dreams, goals, and objectives. To do this you must start where you'll end up; *begin by being there already*. A context is *the whole*; it isn't the activities, the events, the situations, the successes, failures, ups, downs, rights, or wrongs that lie along the path.

When you expand yourself as the context of your life,

you allow life to go on within you. Individual events are unimportant in themselves. The individual events, the point of view you may have as opposed to another's has relatively little if anything to do with your getting there. Within a context of, "I will own the home I love within two years," you will have many ups and downs; you will have doubts and failures as well as certainty and success.

Don't resist good. Without a context that already determines your outcome, you are actually operating against yourself. An example of this is the old context of "the farther ahead I go, the farther behind I get." This *makes* a person fall farther behind, go more in debt, and be more burdened as he or she appears to be moving ahead. This is not inevitable at all. It can all be reversed and cleaned up by the conscious creation of a new context. "The farther ahead I get, the better my life becomes" is a perfect context. If you have resistance to this much good, check into your assumptions and beliefs about yourself and life.

We're working with a force beyond ourselves. We have been given the gift of the Holy Spirit; your good is inevitable, and it waits upon your owning it, your claiming it. The question is, are you willing to let go of your struggle and at the same time practice the principles of life?

SAY WHAT YOU WANT

Let's move along to the fourth aspect of how to get where you want to go. This obviously is connected to the third aspect: You have to ask for and say what you want. Where do you want to go? *Speaking your word declares your intention for yourself*. The context for your life may be, "My life is a manifestation of the Holy Spirit in action." Out of that declaration, everything would be used by the force of life to make this come true.

Tell the truth about your desires. Context creation is the necessary element that uses everything in your life, no matter what it looks like, to help you get what you want. Saying what you want involves telling the truth about your desires. *You* determine the objectives; *you* determine where and what the goal is. Once you say where it is, you must contextualize it—you must be there already. What you've done is expand yourself to include being, doing, and having what you want. An example of saying what you want is, "A job that involves my using my talents fully and contributes to others' lives." To have this you need to accept it as real and true. Expand yourself to be larger than this goal, and include this goal within yourself as complete and achieved. What is left is the process of the seed becoming the plant.

It's time to transcend "time." Time is an element of the physical universe and does not exist in the absolute. At the level of the absolute, time and growth don't exist. It all happens now, in the moment. The closer you live to the absolute, the faster are your manifestations. Time is made up within your mind and as part of the physical universe. What you do when you say what you want and accept yourself is to transcend time. Time actually is used to keep track of what you had, what you have, and what you will have, as well as what you didn't have, don't have, and won't have. Have you ever experienced that part of yourself that remains constant no matter where you are or what you have or how old you are? What changes is the physical stuff. You are still in relationship with everyone you ever were and with everyone who exists, even though their bodies may not even be in your life anymore.

Trust in yourself. Saying what you want requires you to rehabilitate your trust in yourself. What I've realized about myself is that down deep inside I know what I want; my life is a continual process of telling more of the truth about

what that is! The more permission I give myself, the more
I tell the truth.

If you don't know what you want, it's because of one
of three things:

* You were given substitutes for what you really
  wanted.

* You were repressed and held back from being yourself and having what you wanted.

* You were forced to do things against your will.

Don't wait another minute. Practice saying what you
want, observe where it's easy and flows naturally, and notice
if and when you feel forced to be, do, or have certain things
or when you feel inhibited or shut down. Only you can open
yourself up, and that requires your stepping out there. *Waiting hasn't worked; there won't be a magic day when the
real you jumps out there.* You know what you want and
you have to declare that through any resistance. This isn't
about becoming a spoiled child and having tantrums if you
don't get your way. This is a process whereby you tell the
truth to yourself and become open to yourself beyond your
conditioned mind. When you know you can have what you
want, it is easy to support others in having what they want.
I can't explain how it works, but what happens is that
compromise disappears for everyone and everyone gets what
they want. When your wants and desires are fear-based, no
one wins. When they are love- and living-based, everyone
wins.

Don't decide for God. In saying what you want, give up
your expectations about how it's going to come about and
what it will look like. For example, say: "My friends are

loving people who are leaders in business and politics and committed to world peace and transformation." Your declaration, plus your openness and willingness, aligns the forces of life and turns even chance meetings into the miracles that support and fulfill your objective. To have what you say requires that you create it. It is God's power flowing through you; it is God's will manifesting itself as you and your magnificent life. To create it requires that you own it, that you allow it. When someone says, "How do I do it? or "What do I do?" or "Help me to do it," I feel helpless because I don't know how.

You can't do anything for anyone. You can only assist them to be, do, and have *what they are creating.* You must have the experience of causing your reality and the wherewithal to manifest it as part of the growth process. All creation is instant, although it may look as if it takes time. Creation is about your creating as an act of will, not of force. You call it forth from yourself. It isn't you. It is a higher power flowing through you. It is you *knowing* that creation happens out of your saying what you want and calling it forth.

Do what you say. To build your confidence and your experience of trust in yourself and your word, do what you say. By doing the small things—that is, by keeping your agreements, commitments, appointments—the big things look and become easier. If your word is no good, if what you say has no value and no one can count on it, obviously you can't even trust yourself.

BEAR WITNESS TO GOD'S LOVE AND POWER

The fifth aspect of your getting to where you want to go is also to have faith and trust in your own word. This means to set up a plan, if needed, with your goals and "to do" lists. (Remember the value in life is not found in acquiring; it is in the moment-to-moment experience of God's love. It isn't achievement for the sake of achievement or for the sake of proving your worth or value to yourself or another that is important. The true value is your giving witness to God's love and power as it works through you, and *the true miracle is the perfection of it all*. Nothing is denied you, and there is no situation so significant that you should deny yourself love and pleasure.)

Begin step by step—now. So many people are waiting for some big event, their big moment. What a waste, what a shame. They miss out on the celebration of each moment, because each moment is a big event. Again, life is a journey, not a destination. The way you build a house is piece by piece. How you get there from there is step by step. Within the context of "it's done," you then set up a plan to get there, a road map. You could call it a strategic plan, which includes a list of what must be included, considered, and taken care of. You will need a financial plan if finances are part of your goal. You will need a time line and due dates for your intermediate goals. *To say when you are going to do something and actually do it* at that time or before *is a powerful tool*. It's so easy to slide by and put off everything for a future time that never arrives.

DEVELOP HABITS THAT SUPPORT

Your past negative habit patterns, as well as any thoughts of self-sabotage you might have constructed, can't continue in an atmosphere of success. To break an old pattern you must establish a new one. It may be difficult at first, but gradually the new patterns that support you in being, doing, and having what you want are set. We don't want or need to be slaves to habits. Rather, we want our habits to support us and the quality of life we desire. This is the sixth aspect.

Be realistic. Don't set your goals at an unrealistic level for yourself at this time. If they're too high, you could defeat yourself and put yourself down; if they are too low, you could be playing it safe, not demanding enough of yourself. Also, don't use goals and achievements to build or determine your self-esteem and personal worth. That's not the issue.

Movement is the key. If you have large goals and it all seems too overwhelming even to attempt them, do little things that will keep you moving in the right direction and will poke holes in the obstacles to these objectives. Do something every day that is related to your goal and moves you in that direction, even if it's something simple. The more intention, commitment, and action in that direction, the faster you produce results. That which you don't complete each day, put on a "to do" list for the next day. You will make mistakes—inevitably, as far as I know. But don't blame yourself, just discover what works at new levels. Be willing to correct when in error and keep moving.

PUSH THROUGH ALL OBSTACLES

The seventh aspect has to do with the obstacles that will arise. Never stop to "handle" problems or difficult people. Be big enough to include anything, everything, and anyone that comes along in your journey upward.

What look likes obstacles are opportunities to learn. Give up the illusion that you have enemies. The truth has no illusions. It has no obstacles, and it has no opposite. Don't ignore what seems to be an obstacle. Look to see what it's saying, what it wants, and be willing for that person, that challenge, that problem to have what it wants. You may look like someone else's obstacle, but you aren't; just as someone or something may appear that way to you. What is needed may be more information or a higher level of excellence, or perhaps acknowledgment. Ask what the seeming obstacle wants and support it in having that.

Face it and move on. Contrary to popular belief, no one wants what you have, and for sure they don't want to get rid of you or stop you in any way. We make up our enemies out of a desire to play war games. Be willing to confront or face anything, knowing it has no power over you. All that obstacle wants is to go where it's going to get what it wants, and it looks like you are in its way. Obstacles and challenges are opportunities to correct, to let go of something or add to it, depending upon what they're saying to you. *Keep moving. Keep on, and don't wait for permission or the right time.* This takes you where you want to go. Failure to realize this is what actually stops people.

Channel power to the people. People think they are smaller than the trappings in their lives. They give their lives over to fighting midgets that have become giants in their imagination. A river doesn't stop its flow to handle obstructions; it goes over, around, under, or through if necessary. It goes where it's going. It's amazing the sales ability you'd have if you just listened to people's objections until they were through. Their objections usually have nothing to do with whether they'll buy it or not, unless they use that as an opportunity to deny themselves what they really want. After they are finished, ask them which color they like and how many they want. The truth is that everyone wants to have what he or she wants, but many are afraid they'll lose something in the transaction. Actually they gain, not because they are "given" something, but because they have been "empowered." You turn up your ability to channel power by giving yourself and others permission to have more.

Keep loving yourself. Every upset and challenge is an opportunity for more love and more good. Don't use a problem as an opportunity to give up or blame yourself or others. I don't know about you, but I've been a master at heating myself up emotionally by blowing up and making bigger than life and myself something I did or did wrong that was small in itself, and I know it is a mistake to react this way. Instead, look at the whole picture, not just the few pieces you've gathered together to prove something wrong or evil. Look at the whole. Realize and experience the beauty and love that is there. We gather the small part as evidence to try and deny ourselves the good life.

ACKNOWLEDGMENT

Others assist you in "getting there." Without them it wouldn't happen. Even the person who kicked you when you were down did you a favor and assisted you in some way. He or she may have helped you realize you had to get up and do it yourself. That's why the eighth aspect is acknowledgment.

I know it's you who said what you wanted and where you'd go—it wasn't others that did that, it was you. Still, it's all a team affair. Everyone works for everyone else and we are all one. Acknowledge those you feel have contributed and those who are contributing now to your life. To recognize and acknowledge another's contribution is magic for everyone. It keeps the energy flowing. We are dealing with energy flows, inflow and outflow, or the Law of Circulation. What you give out comes back. At first you may be thanking people and acknowledging them because you know they'll keep giving to you. That really isn't it. You are responsible and others are servicing you and helping or assisting you.

Recognize the source. All my glory goes to God, as I of

myself can do nothing. The ultimate source is the higher power. To recognize and praise God and give God the glory is the truth. It isn't the "getting there" that's the issue. It's the recognition of the force that makes it happen effortlessly. We make an effort because we resist effortlessness. Our pain is the result of making a negative thought real. When we try to make ourselves important and significant, we shut ourselves off from others as well as from the force that empowers everything. That force flows naturally; it is blocked when we put our bloated importance in the way.

Real humility is being in awe of God's power as you experience it in action in your life and the lives of others. You aren't supposed to praise God because if you don't you'll go to hell—that's nonsense. Praise is recognizing where the true power is and that it is coming through you and others. You deserve all that God deserves, and that's glorious and beyond our imaginings. If you aren't into acknowledging a higher power, start doing so. That doesn't mean not being responsible for your life; it means recognizing where everything comes from. You receive the gift of life by saying thank you.

In conclusion, don't limit yourself. The limit you feel is self-imposed. You have everything it takes to get where you want to go. It all happens out of you and through your projecting that belief out into life. You are always projecting and reexperiencing the results of that projection, so live what is your heart's desire. To transcend life and move into the realm of living, you must dispense with the mystery of life. To dispense with anything, you have to see it for what it is and recognize that it is no longer a mystery and no longer has power over you. Play the game of life to win, but know that the real winners aren't caught up in the win/

lose game; they are caught up in the challenge and fun of playing. *The reward in life is playing full out.*

Exercises

1. List twenty beliefs you have that keep you from having all the money you need.

2. List ten fears you have about money.

3. Who and what are you afraid you might lose if you become prosperous?

4. What are some thoughts you have about men and money and about women and money?

5. Enjoy your money and enjoy what your money buys. Visualize yourself with all the money you need and want. Enjoy paying your bills and consider it a privilege to be able to play the money game.

6. Examine the strings you attach to money, the meaning and value you attach to it. Let go of using money to manipulate and control yourself and others. Money doesn't mean anything. It's simply an energy flow.

7. List your payoffs in letting money be a problem to you. Are you willing to give up seeing money as a problem?

8. Every time you contribute money, enjoy giving it and affirm that "all that I outflow comes back to me."

Affirmations

I,_____, allow myself to enjoy money and to have what is sufficient for what I want.

I,_____, always have the money to do and have what I choose.

The more money I share the more I receive.

I enjoy giving money and I enjoy receiving money. I enjoy using money.

God is the source of my supply—in this I trust.

I,_____, accept sufficiency for every person on earth.

Money is something of which I have an unlimited supply to do and have what's valuable to me.

The more I give the more I get, and I love to get so I enjoy giving.

* 10 *

Commitment to Commitment: The Key to It All

Everyone is committed to something. The question is: Are you committed to that which nurtures you and gives you what you want in life, or are you committed to that which undermines you and sabotages everything you ever have deeply desired and needed?

The biggest problem with commitment is that for the most part we are not aware of what we are committed to. High intention and commitment is something that is still new to me, and yet in some parts of my life I've been practicing it for years, unconsciously and unintentionally. Commitment for me is a coming together; it is a union. I become one with that to which I am committed. It becomes part of my body—I am it and it is me.

Conscious and high-intended commitment is the missing ingredient in most people's lives. It doesn't mean that there aren't committed people. What is missing is the conscious and *high* commitment that can move mountains, heal the sick, and transform one's life and the quality of life on this earth into heaven.

Nothing Happens Without Commitment

This is the first chapter in the book that I've had to rewrite—the first draft was disjointed, confusing, redundant, and had little impact. That's because the subject of commitment is difficult to get a handle on. It isn't like the topic of money, where you can systematically do the ABC's of finance and produce a specific result. *Commitment is an intangible space from which you live your life.* It isn't a destination, and for sure it isn't an intellectual process. Read this chapter in a way that transcends the words, so that you experience commitment not as a concept, a set of obligations or rules carved in stone, but a quality of being that generates an ongoing process of discovery. I'm going to use words to describe what commitment is and what it isn't, and you must see and hear with other eyes and other ears to catch and embody it.

Out of the commitment from which I live my life, I am up against every belief I've ever had. Every pattern of behavior has to crumble in the face of this greater calling, this greater purpose. Fear is knocking on my door as I keep facing the unknown at the edge. The truth is that, once committed, you can't go back to the illusion that there is something secure in the world on which you can depend and to which you can cling when necessary. This act of commitment—the willingness to live in the unknown and out on the leading edge—may be frightening, but what is true is that my peace of mind grows daily, my sense of security increases, and there is less and less I am attached to. Instead there is expanded love, certainty, and the excitement of living.

THE TWO PARTS OF LIFE

What is apparent to me is that *life is made up of love and contribution lived in a context of commitment*. I was giving a seminar to a few hundred people in Hawaii, and I asked myself why we didn't have thousands of people instead of hundreds. What came to me was that I was unwilling to be loved by that many; I was unwilling to contribute to that many. We had had some misunderstandings and some problems to clean up from the year before, and I had thoughts that I was wrong and bad for not having handled everything impeccably. I judged myself, and in the judgment I blocked receiving love from people and withheld my contribution to their lives, as if my contribution were not of value.

It was my commitment to love and contributing that allowed me to discover how I was blocking myself and others. Out of that experience and realization, I committed myself to allow everyone on this earth to love me and I them, and to contribute and empower every person on this earth. Out of this commitment that will happen—it is happening; it is inevitable. It is the "commitment to the commitment" that will enable me to keep expanding myself and to experience more love and to increase the value, quality, and impact of this message in people's lives everywhere. It is out of this that I become who I am. It's out of *your* commitment that you become who *you* are!

Without commitment nothing happens. That experience

in Hawaii would have been just another event had I not thought realistically about commitment. It allowed that event to make a major contribution to my life and the lives of others. Nothing happens without commitment, and everything happens with it.

FIRST THINGS FIRST

What most people wait for before they commit is what actually occurs after they commit. It is my hope that in this chapter you will discover what you are and are not committed to—and that from this you will discover the value of commitment in such a way as to allow you to fulfill your highest spiritual, mental, and physical aspirations. There will be an opportunity for you to recognize and learn how responsibly to let go of commitments that aren't working for you. Some questions that I'll address are:

* How do I break my word and still know my word is good?

* How long is a commitment?

* What is a commitment, and what isn't?

The biggest obstacle I've had even to considering commitment was my past experience. I had beliefs about duty, responsibility, and obligation that were tied up with my fears of conformity, stagnation, being stuck, immobility, obedience, and terminal boredom. Commitment looked like entrapment and an inevitable prison term and death sentence. It actually seemed like a loss of freedom. Nothing could be further from the truth, for *it actually is in responsibility and commitment that I have found freedom*, life, and the opportunity to fulfill the highest and best within me, as well as within mankind.

What it takes to turn anything around, including the world, is one committed person. You can't be committed only *sometimes*; you either *are* or you *aren't*. The few who know this have accomplished the impossible and the extraordinary. Most people shy away from total commitment to a project, a life-style, a goal, or major objective. Why? They live with misconceptions, underestimating the power within them. They are afraid of failure, of being wrong or rejected. They lack an overwhelming passion for a worthwhile purpose or objective.

Where to Begin

You have to start always from where you are to get where you want to go. If you don't know where you want to go and have no passion for the destination or the journey, you will have great difficulty in just being motivated, let alone in achieving your objective. To begin where you are requires that you examine what you are already committed to and whether those commitments truly serve your purpose and vision. What you are committed to you have become, and out of this your life is shaped.

Take a look at what gets your time, your attention, your thoughts, your words, your actions, your money, and your energy, for that is what you are committed to. *There are empowering commitments and disempowering commitments*. The disempowering commitments drain your vital life force and diminish your opportunity to live an extraordinary life in every way. The empowering commitments augment and transport you into another realm or world of life and living. You become an ordinary person being, doing, and having the extraordinary. In this realm your energy, creativity, love, compassion, talent, health, self-expression, and joy of living are expanded and contributed in a way that inspires others also to live an extraordinary life.

I've listed some disempowering and empowering commitments to assist you in realizing the distinction between the two so that you are able to shift or move yourself where you want to be, if you aren't there already.

DISEMPOWERING COMMITMENTS	EMPOWERING COMMITMENTS
To:	To:
* Avoiding change and living as you always have	* Producing results in a worthwhile project
* Gossip and putdowns	* Ending hunger and starvation
* Self-pity and "poor me" mentality	* Bringing a cure for disease
* Power and cheapness	* Loving and being loved
* Greed and getting money at any price	* Wealth
* Hiding from the truth and pretending there are no problems	* Making your marriage one of love, which inspires others to have loving marriages
* Comfort and no growth	* Creating a loving, supportive family
* "It can't be done."	* World peace
* Staying together no matter what	* Being financially responsible and ethical
* Looking good and keeping up appearances mainly to be accepted by others	* Doing and living God's will
	* Developing your talents and abilities
* Being right and righteous	* Empowering others

DISEMPOWERING COMMITMENTS	EMPOWERING COMMITMENTS
To:	*To*:
* "Ain't it awful!"	* Heaven on earth
* "Someone will save me."	* Physical fitness and a healthy body
* Self-denial	* Transcending aging
* Suffering and sacrifice	* Seeing the value and beauty in every person
* Compromise and selling out yourself and others	* Keeping your word
* Being afraid and helpless	* Surrendering to God's love
* Holding it together for the sake of someone or something	* Being able and responsible
* The past and what's over and gone	* "This moment is it."
* To yesterday being better than now	* Being here in the now and living in the present
* Your poor health and last operation or sore toe	* Contributing fully to others
* Your drama and endless boring stories	* Living fully one hundred percent
* How they did it to you	* Living in beauty
* Being late or arriving early	* Being impeccable
* Being superior and better or inferior and worse	* Telling the truth
* Not being enough or having enough	* Trusting yourself and being able
	* Being true to your ethics, ideals, and principles
	* Having exactly what you want

DISEMPOWERING COMMITMENTS	EMPOWERING COMMITMENTS
To:	*To*:
* "No one loves me, and I'm not worth it."	* Being the one to get the job done
* "I can't have what I want."	* Excellence and quality
* "I'm too old or I'm too young."	* Enriching others
* Letting others do it	* Being a master in your craft or profession
* "Someone should do something."	* Ending war, crime, and disease
* Being tired and exhausted	* One world
* Sleeping	* Your vision, goals, and dreams
* Avoiding responsibility and sliding by	* Practicing the principles of life
* Fighting an enemy	* Being in favor of what you want
* Fighting authority	* Living out on the leading edge
* No solutions and inevitable disaster	* Being committed to personal and global transformation

Use these lists. They should get your wheels turning in such a way as to help you discover your basic commitments. Then let go of the disempowering ones and create and choose the empowering ones. No one can tell *you* what your commitments are. This list is here to help you choose commitments that align with your purpose in life or actually serve

as the avenue through which you realize and fulfill yourself
and your purpose.

What Commitment Is and Isn't

To clarify what commitment is, it is valuable to know
what commitment *isn't*. Here are some examples of the
distinction between a commitment that allows for and demands mobility, expansion, and greater freedom, and a
misbelief about commitment that implies losing freedom,
stagnation, and compromise:

WHAT COMMITMENT IS	WHAT COMMITMENT ISN'T
* A trust	* Duty
* Your word as law	* Obligation
* What you say it is	* Compromise
* What you want it to be	* What others impose on you
* What you use to empower yourself and challenge yourself	* Empty gestures
	* A millstone around your neck
* An agreement	* A method to beat yourself up
* A tool to become what you are capable of becoming	* Entrapment
	* Binding with no exit or opportunity to change
* A statement of what you choose to have your life be about	* Living someone else's plan for you
	* Selling out your vision
* What you use to call forth what is within you	* Being stuck in tradition

WHAT COMMITMENT IS	WHAT COMMITMENT ISN'T
* What you use to catapult yourself way beyond your past experience and where you are now	* Peace at any price
	* Staying as you were
	* Submitting
* Exciting and frightening at the same time	* Forced responsibility
* A "can be" approach to life	* Resignation and forced stagnation
* An expansion and change as you grow	* Holier than thou
* Choosing to surrender to the commitment	
* A tool to get you past the considerations, reactions, and belief in your memory and system	
* A tool to keep you going for your vision, especially when you want to give up, run around, or hide out	
* Taking a stand and being committed to the result completely	
* A tool for you to achieve your true ground of being in God's plan, after which it disappears — you have become it	

You may want to write your own list saying what commitment is and is not to you.

THE CRUCIAL SEPARATOR

The difference between the average person and the great person is in the commitment to life and to living his or her vision. You can have what you want if you are committed to having it. Consider this:

* There are two levels of life: one is material and the other is nonmaterial; commitment works in both.

* If you want something materially, you can have it, and if you want something spiritually, you can have it.

* Your life on all levels occurs out of the stand you take. What keeps people in confusion and ambivalence is waiting for some guarantee before they take a stand, or their unwillingness to declare what their lives are about.

Recently I spent time over lunch with the evangelist Oral Roberts and his wife, Evelyn, at his office in Tulsa, Oklahoma. His ministry is the result of his declaration about his life and work and his planting himself in that spot in Tulsa and going for it. He didn't say, "I'll do this if I get this . . . or if this doesn't happen . . . or if people do such and such." There were no conditions to his taking his stand.

It is absolutely, perfectly okay—even necessary—to "not know" how to do it. The "how to" will come from your declaration and doing what is wanted and needed at each moment. Simply get started now, *today*! You will create and discover what to do, then do that. Some things will work and some won't. In the largest sense, it will all work. In the process you discover yourself, God, and how life works. Without commitment, a person sits and waits for some big event that will give him or her peace, passion, love, wealth, meaning, purpose, and direction to their lives. What you deeply desire is already yours; it is called forth out of the demand you place on yourself.

You discover and experience who you are out of the demand you place upon life through committing to what you want to be, do, and have, especially if it is far beyond what you can manifest at this time. *You can't have a desire without the fulfillment being possible in the idea itself.* My commitments allow me to become what I am capable of being. My trust in God, or the power creator, is intensified out of the achievement of those goals and objectives. Given the magnitude of my intentions, I have to let go of my smallness and my past experience and allow myself to "not know" and to be open to the ways and means that produce those results. It isn't me, it is "the Father within that doeth the works." This is powerful stuff, and you'll only know this through direct experience. To experience it you have to do it!

What Are You Afraid Of?

The fear of commitment is actually the fear of loss and failure on one hand and the fear of gain and success on the other. Losses or gains, successes or failures are all illusions; they are value judgments. People for the most part are stuck between the fear of getting what they want and not getting what they want. Fear of commitment is like that, so look within at any fears you might have about commitment to the quality of your relationships, your purposes, your goals, your objectives, your ideas, your vision. What do you think you could lose? Take a look at commitments you've made in the past and the commitments others have made to you or to your loved ones. Write down your broken commitments, or those important to you that you aren't keeping. Now, *forgive yourself*. You are forgiven, so choose again.

My point is that the best of commitment doesn't work to obliterate grief or the pain of the past. The healing takes place by your allowing yourself to experience that hurt, by either using a partner to talk to and say what you never said before or writing out what you never said or expressed. Once you have faced the hurt and pain of the past and have projected the past into the future, be willing to know that you don't have to sacrifice anything worthwhile to have what you want. *It's a lie that you have to sacrifice anything worthwhile and valuable*. Life always gets better if you will your life to get better. The more I surrender to love and allow myself to be loved, the more I know I never have anything to lose and nothing to gain. All I have is more love and life or less love and life, depending on how open and willing I am. The question again is, are you willing to have what you want? If the answer is yes, you will; if it's maybe or no, you won't.

LOOK AT THE GRASS MORE CLOSELY

"The grass is always greener somewhere else" is one of the biggest roadblocks to making a commitment. "This isn't it" is a common thought. "This is it" is uncommon. Those who live by "this is it" can be happy at any moment they choose and *are* most, if not all, of the time. When you live from "this is it" you are able to experience paradise, love, completeness, satisfaction, and wealth any time and any place. If you are always looking "over there" you will never make "over here" *it*. A commitment requires that you make *this job*, *this relationship*, *this marriage*, *this life* the one you've always wanted. You then *give your all here and now*, and the miracle is here and now, the paradise you have always been seeking. Running from one job to the next never allows you to move beyond the surface into the heart of the opportunity that is there for you to uncover. *Digging deep is the process that reveals the gems.*

"The grass is always greener" is a way of life for some. What rips them off is that they don't go deeper, for example in marriage or relationships, for fear of being hurt. They keep it shallow and keep searching. What they are looking for is someone to love them unconditionally and faithfully. They want a mate who sees their magnificence, applauds the real them, and celebrates their beauty. That person will help them get where they want to go and forgive them immediately, actually never judging them. When searching, *the person you are seeking is yourself*, mirrored in someone else. You attract loving people to be your friends if you are willing to be loved that much *and willing to love others that much*.

We want from others what we don't give to them. You have to *give what you want first*; then it comes back to you.

The Levels of Life

There are an infinite number of levels of love, wealth, and life for you to experience and express. If you stay at one level and leave or get kicked out or left behind every time before you get to the next level, you keep yourself from tasting all the flavors there are. What you seek in the neighbor's yard *is in yours*, if you but prepare the yard, plant the seeds, and then cultivate and enjoy the garden.

What happens is that we get to a certain level and then hit an obstacle or roadblock, or a crisis occurs. We can either spend our energy trying to deal with it, using it finally for an excuse to leave or be left behind, or use the situation to *dissolve the barrier, heal the upset, and move ourselves* to a deeper and more fulfilling experience of love and self-expression. Every moment is an opportunity either to pile on more garbage or to remove the junk from the past and become more alive. Only commitment will allow you to do this. Being aligned with yourself and in favor of really living and being all you can be is the first step if you are to discover your goodness.

It is all yours. You have to claim it right where you are. When I get stuck, I turn it over to God and dedicate the situation to love and peace. I let go of my expectations and my need to control and manipulate, and along comes the miracle. The secret lies in dedicating to love and peace and being willing for love to be present.

What If Things Are "Not Working"?

About this time—if you are in a miserable marriage, a stifling job situation, or involved in a project that's going downhill fast—you may be saying, "Terry, wait just a minute. I *have* been committed and it isn't working! What do I do?" I have no advice for you, no system of do's and don'ts for you to follow. It is all up to you. Only you know if it isn't working. Look within and discover the truth. Do you want to be with this person, do you want to be in that job, do you want to have your project succeed? Get to the heart of it. Does it fit you, is it you, is it what you are committed to for no other reason than *that is what you choose to do*?

In this process you'll clean up a lot. You'll unburden

yourself of all the stuff that you've been dragging with you and carrying on your shoulders. *Commitment isn't burden; it's a choice and a tool.*

AN IMPORTANT TRUTH

The truth is, *no goal or objective is intrinsically better or worse than another.* It isn't better or worse either to stay there or leave. The issue is, are you running, avoiding, blaming, and being irresponsible and disempowering to others? A clean resolve is empowering; an unclean one puts more weight on everyone.

To move on, it is important to examine your original agreement or commitment. In doing this you may be surprised to find that it has been completed or that it was based on fear and scarcity, not love and wealth. Try these steps:

* *Look to see if you can recreate commitment and rediscover the vision and the joy that was there. It could be that you have lost your original vision in the everyday ritual of life—forgotten why you married, why you took that job, etc. Choose that purpose again and recapture the passion.*

* *Get help from people who can assist you in getting back on the track. Clear up the communications with your mate, coworkers, organization, or whomever. The assistance could come through a therapist, spiritual teacher, counselor, or good friend who will tell you the truth—someone with whom you feel safe enough to share your truth without reservation. You need to get in touch with your heart and discover what you really want.*

* *If your commitment has completed itself or doesn't support you or the others involved, it's time to move*

*on. Don't hang back out of guilt. Guilt is ugly and
vicious, and it never saves you from anything. Be
willing to acknowledge the completion of your commitment; be willing to change the form of your relationship. Some relationships are there for a
moment, a week, a year, a lifetime, or an eternity.
In God we are all one and all related as one. In
this world it looks as if we are separate and apart,
but this is surely an illusion. We also love one another, as we are each other. Every relationship and
every goal and objective is for love and bringing
you back to your power.*

When the value of something is over, be wise enough
to recognize it. Don't use this as an opportunity to hurt
yourself or another. Use completion as an opportunity to
clear up anything that is not complete. Communicate hon-
estly and lovingly. Tell each other the value and lessons
learned, so that the occasion clearly becomes a graduation.
Often, we try to negate the incredible value of what existed
between ourselves and others. You wouldn't be here if it
weren't for that relationship, ideal, project, job goal, or
opportunity. Acknowledge the growth, the love, the learning, and especially the contribution.

The great tendency is to heed the call of the ego and
destroy all the beauty and love by turning everything into
negatives. You are cause, you have chosen this and it can
be turned into a holy experience by allowing it to be a lesson
in love and forgiveness. Even if the others involved don't
take responsibility, the issue is *your life*. Where I can *see*
the value, I *get* the value.

Move into being responsible for handling what needs to
be taken care of with an integrity that aligns with your values
and principles and allows you to feel complete. Nothing is

worth losing your peace of mind. Remember, *what you give out comes back*. Deal with others as you would want to be dealt with. The others may or may not treat you in the same manner.

I've discovered that when I made agreements with and commitments to "sharks," they committed to remaining sharks for a long time, and not just with me. Don't take it personally. Next time, choose partners who are ethical, loving, committed, and responsible and who can get the job done. Turn it over to God's love to heal and handle.

MOVING ON

There is no guarantee of anything being a certain way, but what you can count on *if you are willing* is that each completion moves you to another opportunity that is better and more nearly ideal for you than anything before. *You don't learn less in life*, for as your awareness is cleansed and you accept more of your divine right, you have and experience more beauty, ecstasy, wealth, and power. The investment you make in yourself pays off in dividends that are out of this world.

You can have what you want, it's all here for you, but what is required is for you to *determine what is important to you and commit to that by taking a stand out in front of where you are now*. Allow your commitments to draw the best from you and to transport you into a realm of existence beyond the ordinary.

Exercises

1. Look within yourself to discover that to which you are committed, and write that down on paper.

2. Judging from your past record, in what areas can you always count on yourself?

3. Recall any past failures and disappointments having to do with you and commitment.

4. Write down what you are willing to be committed to and commit to it.

5. List any fears and beliefs you have about commitment.

6. Be willing to discover what commitment is by committing.

Affirmations

I commit to _____.

This is it and I am committed to living my vision.

I allow whatever comes up in my relationships to support more life and love.

* 11 *

Empower Yourself, Not Your Reasons and Excuses

Most everyone has a pocketful of reasons, a hatful of excuses, and a bag full of solutions for just about everything.

A reason is something you make up within yourself to give you a (false) sense of security that you are right. Reasons are drawn from your past experiences; they don't tell the truth about the present or the future; they keep you repeating your past and living from yesterdays.

Justification is putting reasons together to make something false seem true. If it is true, it doesn't need justifying. You don't need to prove an inner experience of truth. *Something either is true or it isn't.*

Everyone has had bad things forced upon them, especially as a child, and yet to use that as an excuse for or against whatever is in your life today is of no value. Reasons and justifications only create bitterness and weakness, which grind into sickness, misery, hostility, and powerlessness in some form or another. This chapter is not about denying your experience or denying the pain or hurt you have experienced. It is about letting that go and moving on to greener pastures. It requires that you grow, become greater than incidents or conditions in your past life. Again, this chapter is dedicated to your having what you want.

How Excuses Disempower

Excuses and justifications are in abundance in most people's lives. And all that talk doesn't make any difference! Things continue on as they were. Reasons and excuses only create more reasons and excuses. Like produces like. Results are produced out of the declaration and intention to produce results. You have what you have because you do, and you don't have what you don't have because you don't— period. All things are as you say they are and no other way. I get to work because I say I'll get to work, and if I'm caught in a snowstorm and I don't make it, somewhere I changed my mind and I simply didn't get there. And if I truly wanted to get there, who knows how I'd do it, but I know I'd get there.

A friend of mine was riding in a sailboat when it tipped over far offshore. The wind came up and the sailboat drifted away from her and left her stranded alone in the sea. She had the immediate realization that she could die, but she also realized that she had a choice—and she chose to live. *At this moment a helicopter spotted her, let down a ladder, and she climbed up to safety.*

This may sound totally strange, but a young woman who was a viewer of my television program was on a hike up in the mountains alone. She was sitting on a rock and reading the Bible right at the part that said even if wild animals were after you, you'd be safe in the power of the Holy Spirit. She looked up and bears were coming toward her in every direction. She knew in that moment she had a choice, and she chose to practice the principles of life, as she said with total faith and trust, "In the name of love go away." *All the bears turned away and left her safe.*

Look at all the times you were committed to doing or having something and you did it right, in spite of everything and anything. You go to work or you don't, you have money or you don't, you are loving or you are not, you do what you say you will or you don't. A person steals cars, and others give a reason for it—"He had a bad childhood," "His father ran out on him," or "He couldn't get a job." If you are the person who steals the car, you are justified for sure because, after all, that rich guy doesn't need the car and can get another one; you've had a hard time and it's owed you—or whatever your justification—but the truth remains that you are a car thief. See if a car cares about the reasons you weren't paying attention behind the wheel or that you didn't have the time to buy gas. Too bad. It's all over, excuses or not. Without reasons and excuses, life becomes very simple: yes or no.

Look at how often you give reasons for such things as buying the house you did, or the car or the clothes. Look at the reasons you give for going on vacation, for making a lot of money, or for breaking up with your boyfriend or girl friend. Take a look at the reasons you give for not selling the products you said you would, for not getting along with your parents, for not weighing what you say you would like to weigh. For example, if your problem is weight, the truth is that your body is exactly the way you want it to be. You really need to stop blaming and hating your body and start loving and praising your body for duplicating your thoughts about what you want your body to be like. All things are as you say they are and no other way. At some point you made a decision about your body and your body is expressing that decision.

My life turned around when I committed to letting go of blame, justification, reasons, and excuses for anything and just accepted responsibility. There is that tendency to want to pull a good reason out of the pocket, but I know if I do I disempower myself.

How to Regain Your Power

To restore yourself to who you are requires that you empower yourself, that you let go of all the forms and methods you use to hold yourself back. Justifying "disempowers" you because in the act of it you deny yourself. There is a loss of energy when you take an attitude of helplessness, "poor me," and "I am the victim of my environment and can't do anything about it."

Things happen in life, or rather within life. There are all kinds of particles and pieces to which we attach meaning. Instead of being responsible for our feelings, our attitudes, and our results, we look around to find a particle to which we can attach the responsibility. If you forget an appointment or a date, you find someone or something to which to attach your reason for not making it to the appointment or date, instead of looking to see what's going on with you about the appointment or the date that caused you to want to miss it. You may be sabotaging yourself or getting even with the person with whom you have the appointment. Perhaps you have something to say to that person that you may be afraid of or uncomfortable about experiencing. To examine your own motives and to discover that the cause lies within you (because it is you) is the key to manifesting your dreams.

Everything we experience, see, sense, or feel is immediately stored in our mental computer and becomes a concept and part of our belief system. The result of this action is that we live our lives out of the past. We link things together and perceive events and happenings as cause and effect. "This happened, so this will happen," or "This didn't happen, and therefore this won't happen." Yet the past only repeats itself if we draw our information out of the past.

I know a woman who for years blamed her problems on being Puerto Rican. The truth is she was hiding behind the excuse that she couldn't do what she wanted and wasn't as good as others because she was Puerto Rican. When she finally let that go, she could see she was using it to limit herself and wallow in self-pity. Today she is an incredibly beautiful woman living her vision because she chose to be responsible for her life and her results.

We tend to add up pieces and make decisions based on those partial elements and the conclusion we've drawn from them. For example: "I am female and my father didn't support me financially and he left my mother. Therefore men don't support women and they leave them. Therefore the man I love won't be good to me and he'll leave me. So I'll have to do it on my own." Even if all those events happened, it's still your reaction to them and evaluation of them that makes the impact upon you. You may be the product of a multitude of decisions that in truth only affect you because you accept, believe, and reinforce them through constant use of them.

To free yourself from the cycle of grinding experience into a series of reasons, excuses, justifications, and beliefs that keep you from living out beyond your mind, be willing to generate what you want. That requires that you be responsible, that you be the cause of your life and your results rather than the effect of them. You are in charge of your world; it isn't in charge of you. God is in control of it all, and it all works perfectly and beautifully when we surrender to that much good.

The Uses of Reasons

What I want to do now is call attention to the way you use excuses and justifications in your life, to assist you in freeing yourself from the habit of using them. Empower yourself, not your reasons, for things are the way you say they are and no other way.

There are two basic excuses; one is Reasons and Excuses To Be, Do, or Have, and the other is Reasons and Excuses Not To Be, Do, or Have. You have to remember that given the way your data-based reactive mind (or some say ego) works usually is to make you right, so your justifications serve that purpose. To give all this up requires that you clearly see the cost. Only one who attacks is afraid of being attacked. Only one who loves lives from trust.

Here's a checklist of justification to avoid. See if you find yourself in here.

REASONS AND EXCUSES TO BE, DO, OR HAVE	REASONS AND EXCUSES NOT TO BE, DO, OR HAVE
* To get the approval of others	* To hide behind them and not live one hundred percent
* To keep others from being angry and rejecting you	* To avoid being responsible

REASONS AND EXCUSES TO BE, DO, OR HAVE	REASONS AND EXCUSES NOT TO BE, DO, OR HAVE
* To look spiritual	* To keep others being responsible to you
* To add substance to your simply wanting to	* To avoid others' rejection and blame
* So you can make your notions, wants, and choices significant and important	* So you don't have to declare yourself and be fully visible
* To keep from having more than others or having less	* So you can avoid criticism and attack from others
* To justify by wanting and having that much good	* So you can indulge in self-pity
* To keep from looking greedy	* To keep yourself dependent
* To avoid responsibility for it being your choice	* Not having to face failure
* To get others to give you money	* To stay in a relationship
	* To keep others around you disempowered
* To avoid telling the truth	* To keep from setting a goal that is bigger than anything before
* To avoid acknowledging how powerful you are	* To avoid being more successful than parents
	* To avoid hurting others

REASONS AND
EXCUSES TO BE, DO,
OR HAVE

* To avoid surrendering
  into love and God's
  pleasure

* To placate "them"

REASONS AND
EXCUSES NOT TO BE,
DO, OR HAVE

* To avoid telling the
  truth

* To avoid being hurt

* To control yourself

* To control others

* To stay in suffering,
  struggle, and lack

* To avoid having it all

* To keep yourself and
  others busy with trivia

* To get attention by
  being the problem

* For fear of making
  mistakes and looking
  like a fool

* To avoid blame

* To keep anger and
  self-pity

* To get even

* To escape

* To avoid
  acknowledging your
  full power, so you
  don't have to be
  powerful and able

* To perpetuate attack

* To have an enemy, so
  you can have a cause
  to fight

* To make life hard so
  you have something to
  overcome and make
  yourself look brave

* To avoid too much
  good, pleasure, and
  love

To overcome excuses and justifications you have to be willing to give up your attachment to what people will think and break the agreements you have made to be less than who you are. You have to consciously choose to operate out on the edge, without anything to hang on to and nowhere to hide. You can't go back into your mother's womb and hide; you must grow up. All the qualities of life worth experiencing are waiting for you when you live out of clarity of vision beyond the muddled mess of reasons.

It takes calling yourself on your reason racket and simply telling the truth: "I did it" or "I didn't," "I want it" or "I don't." To say what we want is a key to mastery of life. One kind of risk taker is the one who chooses to tithe ten percent of his or her income to God's work, simply to experience what happens out of contribution and to discover the value of applying God's laws to one's life. Choosing is empowered by an act of doing that transcends reasonableness and catapults you into a realm of living totally beyond the experience and belief of the vast majority of people. To "have" requires this kind of commitment, which only you can make. Consider the cost of not making that choice. *You can't afford to pay that price*, for the price you pay is your life, your relationships, your health, and the living of your vision.

THE WORLD'S BEST REASON

There is no reason more empowering than "because I choose to." God didn't need justification to create the universe. It was simply His good idea. You are perfect as you are and who you are is enough, just as what you want is valuable and worthy of having, merely because you say it is. Make your declarations and go for it! Correct yourself when in error and get off and move on.

The power is in declaration. Miracles happen in declaration. Being unreasonable is having exactly what you want and not settling for a substitute or whatever you think you have to settle for. Declaring is choosing the highest thoughts. It's living from divine creation. The forces of the universe align behind whatever you declare. Keep saying what you want and eventually, if not sooner, you'll be, do, and have what you say.

As you live from declaration you live apart from the mess of mental confusion; you live out beyond, generating through yourself the life that is rightly yours. It is a truly spiritual experience to be free of negation. We are each gifted with everything we need to live abundantly in all areas of our lives, but we can't have abundance if we live from the misconceptions of the past. Every moment is a fresh beginning; every moment you can begin again. A friend of mine, Jay Clark, wrote a poem for me that says,

> Life is a game and no thing really matters.
> So feel God's pleasure.
> Play—and play as if it matters—
> there are no time outs and you can start over
> whenever you choose.

To declare yourself—your intentions, your life-styles, your objectives—is to open up the floodgates of heaven to you. Life is the way you say it is. It is your mirror. You can live from God's love and wealth right now by declaring it so and *being that* right this moment. The more you live this way, the easier and more natural it becomes. It may be difficult at first, but don't give up. Keep at it. When you experience yourself using reasons, excuses, and justifications, stop and look at what you are doing, tell yourself the real truth, and then declare what you want. *The risk is nothing. The reward is your life.*

* 12 *

Follow Through and Complete What You Start

People who can consistently complete or finish what they start have power. Everyone has good ideas, but many of those good ideas are never put into practice, and relatively few of those that are continue on to completion. People tend to fizzle out on their good ideas. I had just stopped playing the piano the first time I heard this, and I realized suddenly that I rarely if ever completed mastering pieces I started out to play. I found them either too difficult or too boring and lost interest. After that awakening, I forced myself to complete the pieces, even if I missed notes or became bored. I realized that I had a habit of not completing what I started, and it was time to break that habit and create new ones if I was to live the life I desired.

The purpose of life is love and the full actualization of the self. Love is complete in and of itself, and it increases with use, just as our talents and abilities do. The more you bring out that which is within you, the more there is to bring out. <u>Completion is the act that empowers you to actualize your abilities, talents, and lovingness</u>. Your goals and objectives are the stage setting that allows you to experience actualization of the self.

Goals and objectives in and of themselves are merely destination points. As soon as you arrive at one point, you probably will decide upon another goal or objective. This process will go on forever. Its value is that it places demands upon your inner resources that expand you as a person. Life is simply survival or "getting by" when no real demand is placed upon the self. The purpose of your work should be not only survival, but the full actualization of self and of love.

We must cultivate the ability to do what we say we will do. The more consistent the results, the more energy we produce out of our efforts. <u>The completion of a cycle is the beginning point for the next energy flow</u>. When you don't complete your tasks, the energy wanders, with no point on which to settle and reflect itself back to you. Thus you experience energy loss or depletion rather than energy gain and increase. The more energy that flows through you, the more you participate in life. The only way to waste life is not to use it.

How to Become a Completer

Completion is natural. In nature there is a beginning, middle, and end to all forms of life, including human life, and that is a necessary sequence. Yet good and able people everywhere feel stopped, unappreciated, and powerless.

When we have been damaged to the degree that we would rather sit around, sleep, not participate, and procrastinate, it almost seems impossible to marshal our full energy and become self-motivated. But every person is a reservoir of natural resources waiting to be called forth, and transformation is the process that can restore us to love and ability.

Here I want to go over the steps it takes for anyone to regain ability and call forth those resources, so you can get what you want through the act of completion. If you already do this, following these steps will increase the flow of energy in your life even more and allow you to experience greater heights of love and actualization of the self. It will assist you in assisting others. I want to help those who have projects they want to start and complete as well as the person who feels resentment, depression, and anger at life, themselves, and others because it looks as if life isn't working in their favor. I am committed to your being all you can be, living from God's love, wealth, and pleasure. A major key is completion.

FOUR GOOD STEPS

I'm not saying that those who complete what they start are better than those who don't. But completion builds certainty, power, and fulfillment. Completion also allows us to prosper and know what we are able to be, do, and have. You get where you want to go in steps, and you can only get to the next step after you have finished the step you are on.

The First Step

Look at your life and see what you have completed and what is still incomplete. Make a list of what you have completed. It doesn't matter what you write down, from baking a cake and washing the dishes to launching a successful rocket to the moon and back. For a few minutes allow yourself to feel the satisfaction and fulfillment that you experience from each completion. Look back into childhood, high school, college, work, home, projects, whatever, and write down each completion that comes to mind. Do the same for relationships, since you have completed and incompleted relationships as well. Completion means you feel satisfied, whole, and as if nothing is missing.

The Second Step

After you do this, make a list of the incompleted projects and goals in your life. Think about your body, relationships, work, career, finances, and more. If this seems like a major undertaking and you feel overwhelmed at the mere idea of it, that's normal. Get into it.

This isn't to prove you incompetent or to pat you on the back; it's to get you going in the direction you want to go. It's a have-not world because people don't know how to have and how to let go and enjoy the glory of it all. This completion process will go on forever, as you are always starting, continuing and stopping in every stage of your life. One must recognize and acknowledge completion and let go of the thing completed in order to move on.

In the marriage ceremonies that I conduct, I begin by having the couple recognize and acknowledge that they have found their right mate, so that they will fully accept monogamy. Too often we take a "grass is greener" approach, hoping someday, next job, next person, next lifetime everything will be perfect. We put off the experience of *now*, and *having arrived*, in hopes of finding something better.

Completion can bring up fear of death, the fear of the

good coming to an end—or perhaps the fear that you won't have anything more to do or that you won't have any more of anything. All completion means is the end of *one* step; it means nothing else.

In my relationship with my children, Suzanne and Rebecca, I've had to face the end of various levels of that relationship. Each time that happened there was fear and irrational upset about our relationship being over, and yet each time it had to die at that level so that it could be born at the next. When you hang on and refuse to let go and complete, you deny yourself the next existence, which only comes with completion and moving on.

My friends, co-workers, and I continuously go through this process, because we are moving on to new levels of awareness that demand facing and letting go of old beliefs and old patterns in other relationships and, at the same time, choosing to live at higher levels of love, intimacy, sharing, and empowerment.

Completing this book has caused pressure. The illusion is that if I don't complete it, I won't be judged, therefore I won't fail. There is the tendency not to finish because, after all, who can criticize you when you are still working on something? People tend not to let anything go. Have you ever known a pack rat person, one of those who collects and holds on to everything? My great-grandmother Bertha Hall had some friends whose homes I had the opportunity to help clean out when they died. They were loaded with the past. Living in the past is death to the present and future. The less you complete *now*, the less energy, clarity, power, and enthusiasm you will have.

Let's go back to our list of incomplete projects and goals. *Cross off everything you no longer choose to have*. It's okay to change your mind. For completion, all that is required is to give yourself permission to no longer want something and to let go of it. This can release a tremendous amount of energy. Now *get rid of anything you no longer want*. For example, if you aren't going to reupholster that sofa, call someone to haul it off. The act of letting go is where the power is, not in the list or the talking and thinking about it. *Get rid of it now, today!*

I gave my new, expensive sewing machine to my daughter, Rebecca, and when I did my small self said, "You'd better not give that away. It's expensive and you might sew again one day." The truth was that I did not want to sew again, and why hold on to a past era? I decided that I like clothes made by others and that I will always have the money to buy what I want, even a new sewing machine if I choose. That act in itself closed the door to my past poverty consciousness regarding clothes. I had not chosen to sew to master a craft. I sewed because I didn't believe I could buy what I wanted. What opened up for me was moving to a new level of prosperity and a new level of clothes.

Give up all that drains you, what you feel you "should do" or should hang on to. Do whatever it takes to close the door on it. It may mean that you have to go to your father and say, "Dad, I don't want to do or have such-and-such, and so I'm saying good-bye to it." Often our desire for other people's approval and acceptance, as well as the belief in scarcity, contributes to our incompleteness. Nothing empowers you like doing exactly what you want. What can keep you from being empowered is the belief that you can't be trusted with that much freedom or that you won't be motivated to be a good person or work hard if life goes your way.

People are naturally motivated when they are restored to their natural high. Life is an adventure and a glorious opportunity to express yourself and enjoy.

The Third Step

Make a list of those items you want completed but don't want to do yourself. Hire someone or delegate the task to another to complete. That is still doing it—you are simply leveraging yourself through another. That is the true secret of a successful leader, entrepreneur, or manager. You empower others, especially if it's their gift and talent to follow through and complete your ideas and projects. Everyone wins.

The Fourth Step

Now make a list of what you want to complete yourself. It may be letters to write, a closet to clean, a book to finish, or a car to fully clean and repair. Power, renewed vitality, and enthusiasm for life will leap out at the completion point.

The Problem of Feeling "Forced"

As children, many of us shut down on the joy of work and doing things for the fulfillment and satisfaction of it. If you feel that you were forced to work or forced to do things, you will shut down, and anger will mount like a steam engine. A big *no* and wall of resistance are always there. You must try to overcome that. Look to see who forced you to work or do something you didn't want to; reexperience how you felt, the decisions you made, and how all this affected your life.

Open yourself up again by seeing that it was you who shut yourself down and you who paid the price. We can blame others all we want, but the truth remains that it is your life and we can't shut anything down without shutting ourselves off. *To be righteous and stubborn is the death blow of creativity and of full self-expression and love.*

Produce results out of choice. If you don't have the job of your choice, it's probably because you don't consistently produce results. You produce results out of consistently completing what you start. You start, you follow through, and you complete. You then go on to the next thing—you start it, follow it through, and continue its progress to completion and so on.

I hire people because I can count on them consistently to support me in accomplishing what I want to, and I, in turn, support them in accomplishing what they want to. Feeling sorry for someone is not a reason to marry or hire them. People who can consistently produce results are invaluable. Most people go to work because they need a job, but they're not fully there. Their minds are somewhere else. They often feel victimized by the organization or life itself, and yet all the time they have the power to have it all and enjoy it all.

The trick is to start now. The satisfaction and fulfillment of having your ideas become real and tangible is an incredible high. *Experience your value to yourself and others.* Then you will no longer live in fear of losing a job or losing the life you desire, because you know the principles and use them.

You may want to start small, but *start now.* Do whatever it takes to press past wanting to stop and wanting to quit. You'll probably drag up every excuse not to follow through. If you can't follow through yourself, get it done by having someone do it for you. Finish painting that bureau, and make it excellent. <u>Excellence always produces wealth</u>; wealth doesn't always produce excellence. Excellence produces self-esteem and personal value. The truth is you are valuable just being you. The experience of value comes from recognizing, "I make a difference. I make a contribution and I produce results."

There's no limit as to what you can experience of your talent and ability, and there is no limit to the quality of life you can achieve and experience simply by following through and completing what you start. The masters are not the idea people. Everyone has ideas—everyone's going to write a book, everyone has an invention that could make a million, and everyone deserves to live fully and prosper mightily. Why do only a few make it? Because they start, follow through on, and complete making their ideas reality; they discover that *the power is in the completion*.

Exercises

1. Write a list of what is incomplete in your life (projects, relationships, etc.).
   a. Let go of what you have no intention of completing and cross it off the list.
   b. Put an X next to every *incomplete* that you want to complete and that you will turn over to another to do. (Pay them for it if necessary.)
   c. Put an O next to every *incomplete* that you will complete yourself. Note a date for completion and finish it.

2. Make a "to do" list each day, and check off each item completed. The completion increases your energy and your faith in your ability to do what you say you will.

3. If you are having difficulty completing or finishing something, ask yourself these questions and write down every answer or thought that comes forth:

    a. What is keeping me from completing this?

    b. What am I avoiding facing by not completing this (or what comes next after this project)?

    c. What does completion mean to me, and what am I afraid of in completing?

4. Make a list of everything you can recall you have completed and notice the energy you feel. Acknowledge yourself every time you complete anything, no matter how routine or small.

Affirmations

I,_____, enjoy completion.

Everything I,_____, complete brings more good into my life.

I give myself permission to complete and move on to my next adventure.

I,_____, can complete without the fear of loss or dying.

I,_____, consistently complete what I start with pleasure.

* 13 *

Get Rid of What You Don't Want

To be able to get rid of what you don't want is just as important as being able to create what you do want! Nothing is more frustrating than to be stuck with something you'd like to be rid of, whether it be an unhappy relationship, an attitude that weighs you down, or crime in the streets. What traps most people is that they are not aware that they have the ability to get rid of things, so they are left with resisting problems, fighting them, trying to destroy them, ignoring them, forgetting them, putting up with them, hoping they go away, coping, pretending something didn't happen or doesn't exist, justifying it, or blaming it.

There is a code in this world that says, "What you resist persists." The Bible says, "Resist not evil." You will observe a lot of resistance to something or someone as you look into your life or the lives of others.

Have you ever wondered why, with all the causes and committed people and organizations dedicated to fighting evil of one sort or another, evil is still thriving and going strong? We fight crime, war, bad people, poverty, wealth, divorce, pollution, you name it. Have you ever noticed how much of your time, energy, talent, and money is invested in trying to prevent something you don't want from happening or in stopping an enemy of one kind or another?

To get rid of something, cease to be a party to its manufacture. The very thing you don't want is there because you are giving it its life and power through your attention and energy. We become like that which we resist. It won't be there if you turn off the energy flow in that direction.

An enemy can only be an enemy if it is considered an enemy. Stay with me if this doesn't make sense to you at this time, because I'm sure you have many questions. If people would give their attention and energy to what they want and what they have that they want, instead of putting it on what they *don't* want, they'd have *more* of what they want.

What you give your attention to increases because it's your attention that actually feeds it.

If you give your energy and attention to creating and having a beautiful life and beautiful world, you can spend your time and effort doing and having just that. I'm not saying to ignore what looks like trouble or a potential danger. I don't mean putting your head in the sand like an ostrich. Be aware and choose where you project your energy.

Recognize That You Created It

To get rid of what you don't want, you must first realize that at some time or other it didn't exist, then came into being. It came into being for you because you allowed it, agreed to it—in essence, created it. You may have forgotten that you did so, but if it's in your life, you put it there and you are still creating. *You are working in opposition to yourself.* It is like two people pushing with equal power on opposite sides of a swinging door. Nothing happens; the door stays where it is.

RELATIONSHIPS

Say, for instance, that you have a relationship in which you feel stopped and suppressed. You are fighting it; you don't want it and resent it. You probably spend a lot of time trying to get the other person to stop impeding and suppressing you. You may even blame yourself for not being better, more loving, and positive so you can help. Your energy and self-image around that person probably swing like a yo-yo as you focus energy and attention on trying to resolve the relationship problem.

Look inside yourself and realize that somewhere, sometime you made a decision to put *yourself* down or to save someone by putting *yourself* down. You decided you couldn't have love and that you weren't worthy of support. At some moment you chose to create a way to punish yourself and keep yourself from having too much good. You may have decided that to be a good person you had to suffer and be with a bad person. What's true is that you chose it and are still choosing it, but now you are resisting your own creation. If you don't realize this, you may get rid of the person who is stopping you, but you will soon find another just like him or her. As long as such a situation goes on, you are giving energy to its creation at some level. To stop this, realize that you are choosing this and then free yourself.

MONEY

If you have a money problem, instead of resisting the problem and believing money or others to be at fault, look at the decisions you have made about money, wealth, and poverty. People tend to stay on the surface and deal with conditions rather than look to the cause of their conditions. Often they decide upon a course of action based on scarcity, fear, or loneliness.

FAMILY

If you have a parent problem that you've been trying to stop, prevent, or get rid of, rather than trying to change yourself or your parent, look at the decisions you've made about yourself and your parents. You will find that somewhere you made a decision about them that helped create the problem. It could have been "I'll never be right with them." If that was it, you are trying to "be right with them" and failing because you have the prior idea of "I'll never be right with them" still manifesting itself.

CHILDREN'S BEHAVIOR

You could have a problem with a disobedient child. The child's behavior upsets you, and you spend time and energy trying to stop the child from being disobedient. I would guess that you threaten a lot or try new techniques in child psychology. If so, you are resisting, instead of looking within yourself to discover that you made a decision at some point that is still being energized. You could be recreating a pattern that started when you were a child. Often, a parent is afraid that a child will be bad, that failure as a parent is imminent. Often it's the belief system we have or the value judgments we have made that are being challenged or stressed. It could be that those judgments may no longer be valid (if they ever were), and yet you are in a showdown with your child on who is right and who is wrong. If the child gives in to you, you both lose; if you give in, you both lose. Again, first realize that the condition is there out of your creating it on some level, so choose a good condition instead of resisting one that won't work for you.

Learn to "Let It Be"

A big step in getting rid of something is to let it be. That means: *Allow this condition to exist rather than fighting it.* If you are depressed, give yourself permission to experience depression. You are choosing depression (we'll get into that later), so be true to yourself and experience it. Instead of resisting or fighting the imagined obstacle or the other person's opinion, allow it to be a part of the whole picture.

If you believe you weigh more or less than you should (and remember "should" is a value judgment), choose that weight rather than resist it. Then allow for it, accept it, and be comfortable with it. At some point you chose to be what you call fat or thin—you made a conscious decision about your body and weight. Stop trying to pretend you are a victim, and surrender to the truth by consciously choosing to weigh exactly what you weigh and allowing yourself and your body to be perfect exactly as you are.

Find out when you decided. Look into your life and discover the time and place and situation where you made that decision about whatever you have in your life that you want to disappear. If you don't seem able to do that, your alternative is to allow the full experience of whatever you are resisting and then to choose again. Choose afresh what you want now. (We take care of that in another chapter. For now I want to be thorough in helping you get rid of what you don't want.)

Don't stop yourself. Nonresistance is also "turn the other cheek" as taught in the Bible. When you fight something, you give it power; it flourishes as result of your attention. If you don't want people to criticize you and you run around trying to stop criticism and judgment, you in effect are letting yourself be run by other people. If you are trying to stop people from leaving you or talking about you or appreciating others, to some degree your life is taken up doing this, and still you can't stop it. *What you stop is yourself having what you truly want.* Remember this: The energy you put on stopping someone or something stops you. If you successfully stop anything by whatever means, it will inevitably pop up again, for you need an enemy to prove your point.

Some people actually live their lives out of opposing or avoiding opposition. *Put your energy on creating what you want, not on stopping what you don't.* If your energy is put on stopping your mate from leaving you, you live in fear, and that can actually drive him or her away. More importantly, you cut yourself off from love. The truth is that you already have what you want—love and capability. God loves you, the universe supports you, and everything is here for you. Only you can deny it by making up an enemy.

Know there are no enemies. Creating an enemy is the work of the ego—the false self—to make yourself significant and important. No one can stop me, for I am totally empowered by life itself to fully express and contribute the talents in me into life. I have no enemies, for I see myself in others. I love others and do not attack. I know what people really want: love, to live their vision, and to contribute and be admired for their contribution.

Devalue What You Don't Want

Give up the value *in having* the person or condition you say you want to get rid of. If I choose to let go of depression as a way of life, as I did, I have to give up the value I imagine I receive from it. For me the value was that I could play a self-pitying, helpless "poor me" game and thereby control someone. To release yourself truly from a clinging attachment to other people and things is freedom. It's amazing and disturbing to look back and see what I did in order to dominate or control others.

When you forget that it is *you* who is creating your reality or life, you look to others as your source. The fear of loss is the hidden motivation for most such behavior; that is why we resist or fight what we don't want. We believe that we can be overwhelmed or consumed and that what we hold dear will be taken away. It's a wonderful experience not to have anything, so that you can truly experience how beautiful you are and that life is not about possessing. Then you are free to live and to let go at will.

Again, look at the value you receive out of your fight, out of your opposition, out of the condition you say you no longer want. The truth is that when you no longer want it for any purpose and are ready to give it up, you won't have it. It will disappear.

"HANGING ON" OUT OF FEAR

There are people who are afraid to let anything go because they have attached themselves to a thing or condition and actually are afraid of losing a part of themselves if they discard it. They believe that something is better than nothing, even if that something is killing them. People are actually dying to get out of relationships but stay because they are afraid they can't find another one that is better. People actually allow their jobs to create sickness and death rather than choose another job that allows for more joy and aliveness. Not to know that you have the power to start over every moment and have what you want, not to be able to get rid of what you no longer want, turns you into a victim of life. The result is deadness, low energy, anger, hostility, compromise, sellout, apathy, and all other forms of powerlessness. Only you can blow the whistle on yourself and give up playing a no-win game.

Look deeper than you have. If you don't want to be sick, then give up the value or payoff in being sick. You may say, "I don't *get* any payoff or value! I just can't *help* it." Look deeper. You may have adopted the illness from a family member or close friend you admired or loved and are acknowledging your love by taking on that person's burden.

You may believe that you are unable to care for yourself, so you have an excuse for insisting others more able than you be responsible for you. You may have tried to help someone and failed, so you took on his or her ailments. You have to agree to take on something, or else it can't stick to you. At our deepest level we need to realize that suffering and denial of life at any level is not what love demands. Love demands that you be all you are capable of being without sacrifice to yourself or another.

Give up the fear of loss. When I know the value I get from resisting what I don't want and yet still cling to it, I realize that I'm doing this to hold myself back or to stop another from being all he or she can be. We must transcend the fear of loss by actually living out on the leading edge of creation, continuously letting go of what no longer supports us, continuously letting go of the urge to fight another or resist another's attack. To live in the realm of creation is to be alive and joyous.

We were born into a world of violence created out of the fear of scarcity and loss. Look at how history repeats itself, even with all our good intentions. A radical departure is needed at the level of the self or the core being. To transform your life and the quality of life around you requires that you put this realization to work and prove its workability through your experience.

To Sum Up...

To get rid of what you don't want demands that you withdraw your attention and your power from it and be willing to see it for what it is: nothing. If you had no war to fight and no enemy, how would you live your life? When the temptation comes to resist, to fight, to hold on, take that opportunity to let go. Don't give your energy to it or muster up for war and attack. Simply let the situation be; even allow people to play themselves out. Declare the truth, which is that no one and no thing can stop you from living your life fully.

This doesn't mean becoming a doormat. Plainly and simply, if you really don't want something, stop creating it. If you still hang on to it, that's perfectly all right; just be aware that *it is you doing this*. Otherwise you remain a helpless victim belittled by the users of the world you have created. God is limitless, and so are you.

Exercises

1. *Choose what you have*. Totally accept where you are and give up all your resistance. Simply be in the moment and consciously say, "I have exactly what I want. This is it, and I feel satisfied and complete."

2. Clean out your closets, home, garage, automobile, office, and desk. Give or throw away everything that isn't exactly what you want.

3. Observe what you are being, doing, or having in your life that you don't want.
   a. Why do you hang on to it?
   b. What's your payoff in holding on to it?
   c. What are you afraid of if you stop it or let go of it?
   d. What does it cost to hang on to it?

Affirmations

I,_____, can change my mind and change my life any time I choose—it's my right.

It's my life and I, _____, now easily let go of anything that I don't like or want.

Letting go is natural and allows me, _____, and others to experience more love and more joy.

I, _____, forgive myself for letting go of what others think I shouldn't.

I, _____, can let go of thoughts, beliefs, customs, things, and people with love and accept my new life now.

Others can let go of me, _____, and I am released to more love.

I forgive others who have let me go, and I, _____, thank them for moving me along to more good.

I, _____, allow life to flow through me as I flow through life.

* 14 *

What You Admire and Acknowledge Increases

When you fight someone or something, you give your power to it, and the power you let flow to it increases it, whatever it is. But when you let admiration and love flow out, miracles happen. If you were to flow admiration to your enemy, finding something that the two of you have in common, that person could be transformed into a friend. The truth is we are all one at the level of who we are. Our true differences are not conflicting, but actually supportive. The problems lie at the level of our egos, which create our fears of scarcity and loss.

To let admiration flow out is to live from the core of truth and love. The more you let love and admiration flow, the more love and admiration you actually experience.

When you give your attention to all that you believe can harm you or hurt you, you actually are giving it substance.

What you are saying with your attention is, "This is real. If I don't stop it, it will take away what I want, keep me from having what I want, or hurt and destroy me." When you give something your attention you are actually saying, "This is important to me," either as what you don't want or as what you *do* want. It is the direction and intention of this flow that produces the result.

Use energy to "start" something. Using energy to create what you *do* want is altogether different. When you take care of what you have, you set yourself up for more. When you neglect what you have, you lose even that. Lack of attention results in deterioration.

I knew a man who could only condemn, criticize, and attack. He was a magnificent person underneath it all, just as is everyone, but out of his fear of being condemned and attacked, he developed a defense system. He did this to render others powerless so they couldn't hurt him. He is a suppressive person, and life around him has deteriorated. He can't keep jobs, he can't have nurturing relationships; material things fall apart and finances don't work. He makes a first impression as one who has style, charm, and positive power, but his relationships go downhill from there. This man craves love and success but drives it away out of his terror.

Reverse the energy flow. "Getting" doesn't exist; it's an illusion. Everything you think you "get" gives you only a moment's high, if that. What you need is to turn around and go in the opposite direction, reversing the flow of energy toward the positive. You may have to do this on faith as an act of courage, until you experience the inner value. Sometimes we turn our lives around because of an inner experience that tells us this is the direction we must go in, even when there is no evidence in our lives to support this new direction. To let admiration flow out to someone or something that isn't giving you what you want requires giving up your righteousness, your pride, and your demand that the other person love and admire you first.

How to Start the Outflow

First, remember the Golden Rule and the two great commandments Jesus gave us: "Thou shalt love the Lord thy God with all thy heart, and with all thy soul, and with all thy mind," and "Thou shalt love thy neighbor as thyself." Then try some of the methods that follow to open up life by letting admiration flow out.

STEWARDSHIP

Take care of what you have. For example, instead of swearing at your automobile and mistreating it, start blessing and praising it. Take care of it and treat it as you would a quality vehicle. That doesn't mean you need to be preoccupied with material things, but it does mean being a good steward. That is life-affirming. *The more you affirm life, the more life is worth affirming.*

What is the fear that causes us to withhold admiration and acknowledgment? As I have looked within myself (within is where you find the answers to your questions), I have discovered a fear of loss. If I love and admire something, I could lose it. If I admire my mate and acknowledge him, he will become so magnificent and believe so much in himself that he won't want me. If I take care of and admire and appreciate what I have, I might not get anything else. If I am satisfied and happy with myself, with you, and with what I have, why would I need or want anything else? I'd have no reason or motivation to improve my talents or change things in myself. If I admire you and accept you as you are, how will I get you to stop doing what I don't like, and how will I get you to be what I want?

The refusal to acknowledge or express admiration is a great ego trip and actually *produces the very thing we fear*. We must abandon living in the past or the future in a context of scarcity and embrace living in the present in a context of sufficiency and wholeness. We choose what we have. The most valuable gift we can give ourselves, besides love, is to accept and acknowledge that we always have what we want. This does not take away our power to change or alter what we do or don't have.

To choose is to choose, and we don't need a reason for this. We don't need to prove how badly off we are or how miserable and sick we are in order to justify choosing again. Look within yourself and see if you have any fear of accepting, admiring, and acknowledging yourself and others. Make sure you are not pretending or denying. Let admiration flow out, and you empower others not to need you.

PRACTICE

Practice letting admiration flow out to every person you meet. Open up your heart. Like others and see their value beyond any appearances. Know that where they are and the way they are is exactly where they need to be in their process of healing and awakening. Life is perfect exactly the way it is. To withhold admiration is to deny this truth and shut yourself off from your own good. *Judgment of yourself is the motivating force in your judging others*. To make yourself imperfect is to deny yourself God's love and admiration. Withholding admiration is an attempt to punish yourself. It doesn't work!

To admire someone doesn't mean you necessarily want

to have a relationship with them, lend them money, hire them to work with you, vote them into public office, or marry them. One of the fears about offering admiration and acknowledgment is that it may involve commitment on your part or the other person's. People are so love-starved and spiritually deprived that they either run from admiration out of fear that you may want something from them or will hurt them, or they grab on to you thinking you will take care of them or give them something they believe they don't have.

FORGIVE—AND EARN TRUST

One of the great lessons I learned recently was discovering the difference between knowing who someone is and trusting them to do a job responsibly. The difference is this: Every person is a lovable, able being, whether or not he or she knows it. A loving, aware person knows this to be true. However, because most people are not living out their lives at a level of responsibility, integrity, and awareness, some people are not trustworthy. People have to earn the right to be trusted. This does not create a problem when you realize it, because you then allow people to be untrustworthy or irresponsible while knowing it isn't personal.

Each of us has to become responsible for creating our own results. Problems arise only if you make a big deal out of people being irresponsible and use that to undermine them. Other problems arise when we try to keep people small by giving them only responsibilities that are small. You have to give them room to grow and to come up to their power. The way to handle this is to create the opportunity for communication, so they feel safe telling you the truth about their mistakes or lack of integrity and thus can be responsible at the level of where they are. Forgiveness and acceptance are empowering, except when you keep forgiving someone who doesn't show a willingness to become responsible. Then you are being a sucker and playing a victim number.

CREATE

You must create and generate the context of your life out of nothing. If you don't generate it by acknowledging who you are and that God's love and wealth is yours always, you will live in a world devoid of love and wealth. *You have to call it forth, declare it, or it isn't for you.* The goodies are available outside the realm of your belief and concepts about life. They occur in the realm of your experience moment to moment. You literally must begin fresh every moment. If you operate from past hurt, beliefs, events, circumstances, and experience, it is impossible to turn around and start afresh. The past holds no value except the love that was there and the discoveries you made about yourself and life.

Who and What to Admire

To let admiration flow out is to experience directly that God's love and life flow out from you and is the actual experience you have been seeking.

Take a look at the people, places, and things you have been complaining about, negating, fighting, and fearing. Write down a list of those you recall, and then begin the process of wishing them well. Actually visualize them as happy, loved, and successful. See them prosper and be admired. If you believe there is a scarcity of admiration, you may withhold admiration so that there will be some left for you. *It doesn't work that way!* Look for something within all those negatives you have written down that you can love and even agree with.

Start with those you've been blaming. I remember the first time I had credit cards in my name as a single woman. That was a big step for me; it meant I was responsible and able to take care of myself. But I kept bad-mouthing credit cards about being too much of a temptation. The result was that one of my credit-cards was canceled, and no matter to whom I talked at that company, I couldn't get my card back. I realized I was afraid I'd be irresponsible with the card, which I had been in years past. I blamed the credit card companies for my *own* irresponsibility, so naturally I set myself up for trouble from them. Look on the other side of blaming another. You may find that *you* have done something that wasn't okay or that you failed to do something you should have. As soon as I realized what I was doing, I started appreciating credit cards. I chose to be responsible with them and play by their rules. I value our relationship and acknowledge the service they offer me.

Move to your own body. As another example, if you negate your body, it will negate you. Negation doesn't produce an affirmative. Let admiration flow energy into your body. Notice every part of your body and appreciate and acknowledge how it serves you as the temple of the Living Spirit. Bless your body, love your body, and admire your body. Your body is your idea of what your body is to you. Your body is here to serve you. Instead of condemning it, admire and acknowledge it.

Include your offspring. Admire your children. Look at their faces, hair, bodies, and just admire them, without judgment or expectations. Be willing for them to live their way and not your way. Stop using negation as a tool to shape them up—or anyone, for that matter. Admiration does not mean that you agree with everything. To admire is to appreciate who a person is and to grant him or her beinghood and value.

Add your coworkers. Admire the people with whom you work. If you are working with an extremely difficult person, even if it's your boss, start letting admiration and acknowledgment flow out to him or her. Visualize that person as being more successful, happier, and more loved. Truly be there to support him or her in having everything he or she wants. You will see people being transformed before your very eyes. And you will benefit as you open yourself to admiration and acknowledgment. You are denied nothing, and no one is out to harm you. It's what you give out that comes back.

It's Your Choice

It seems to me that many people like their dramas, upsets, and crises more than having a glorious life. Everyone has the choice. Admire trees, plants, animals, other races of people, people of other religions, old people, ex-mates, ex-bosses, money, your competition in business, beautiful people, wealthy people, poor people, beautiful things, and more. Appreciate what is around you.

Admire this moment, this day. Be grateful and give the glory to God for all your good. If you don't think you have any good, that's why you don't have any. Find something to be grateful for and start admiring it, agreeing that it is valuable. Pay attention to people, listen to them and hear what they are really saying. Find something to acknowledge them for and let your admiration flow to them. To do this oftens means overcoming pettiness, righteousness, or fear of disapproval. It also requires that you give up any fear that life without drama, upsets, or crisis is boring.

If you admire all of life, all of life will admire and acknowledge you.

Exercises

1. Make a list of everything that you do not like or admire about yourself: your body, personality, qualities, ways of dealing with others, etc. No part of you is too small to ignore.

2. Begin a lifetime process of admiration by going over everything on that list and consciously admiring, liking, accepting, praising, and acknowledging it.

3. Observe how you control yourself and others through put-downs, criticism, complaining, and gossip! Observe how you let others control you through criticism.

4. How would you be, talk, think, and behave if you lived from praise and acknowledgment? Visualize and *feel* it!

Affirmations

I, _____, look for the good in everything and praise it.

Everything I, _____, praise and bless, blesses and enriches me.

Every word I speak is a contribution of love and empowerment to myself and others.

The more I, _____, give my energy to what I want, the more what I don't want disappears.

I, _____, praise and admire easily and give the glory to
   God.

It's okay for me, _____, to admire and love my body.

My body is beautiful, and so am I.

****

Don't Worry;
It's Working!

****

* 15 *

Falling Apart Is
Falling Together

When I first started consciously using my ability to create, I used it to hold my life together, to actually prevent what I didn't want from happening. I used visualization, affirmations, positive thinking, and any manipulative technique I could get my hands on to hold people in place and to keep things looking good. I even used prayer to stop the worst from happening and to perpetuate my false need to be in charge. But no matter how hard I tried, I couldn't hold anything together—my life kept falling apart. I'd desperately do whatever I could to pull it back together and prevent what I didn't want to face or deal with. Of course, what kept happening was what I didn't want to face or deal with.

Just about everything fell apart—if not completely, it teetered right on the edge. I would get one thing back on track and then have to run to keep something else from falling. I felt like the juggler on the "Ed Sullivan Show" who kept all those ceramic plates spinning on the tops of poles. He'd have to keep all ten of them going at the same time or else, one by one, they'd fall and break. If you've operated like this, you know the feelings of frustration, fear, and upset it causes. I sometimes felt as if I couldn't leave the house because my kids and husband at the time would harm each other if I were not there to keep the peace. I felt they all needed my attention every moment. If they didn't get it, I would be punished, and my world would again fall apart.

My usual reaction after anger was to go to my room, lie face down on the bed, and cry, "Why me? Why does this have to happen? Why can't everything work?" Today, as I write this, that is as far from my experience as if it were in another lifetime. What happened is that little by little I let go and stopped being responsible for everybody's life and for everybody's feelings. Most importantly, I gave up trying to stop the process of life from happening.

Upsets are opportunities for a healing to take place. They are opportunities to communicate and to let go of what no longer works or may never have worked. *And you don't need upsets to grow.*

In the process of life, we either add to our collection of hurts, misunderstandings, and limitations in some form, or we let go of the ones we have and become more alive. An untransformed person gets worse off as he or she gets older. Transformed people become better off as they get older. A clearing away and a restoration take place that allow us to become more of what we already are naturally. I call it going home, like the Bible story of the prodigal son. We have learned so much that isn't true, and we have so many patterns of behavior and filters through which we perceive life that are based on fear and untruths.

The big barrier for me has been, "What will people think or say?" I bought the whole package about being a success and looking good to others. To me that meant having a husband and having kids who were pretty, talented, obedient, and well behaved. It meant living in a nice house in a nice neighborhood and having everyone say, "Isn't she a nice person" and "Look how perfect her life is." This meant, of course, that I couldn't be angry, that I couldn't have problems, and that I always had to be nice. Isn't *nice* a nothing word? It has no commitment. It just lies there. I basically closed the lid on myself, nailed my own coffin shut.

What saved me was an inner desire to live. I got to the point where I knew I was dying as I was, so I had nothing to lose if I were killed "out there" in the big world. That sense of being dead may seem like an exaggeration to you, but it really was just like that for me.

Falling Apart Is Okay

Falling apart doesn't always mean big tumult. It can be something as simple as looking at the way you do your work or play a game of tennis or golf and realizing it doesn't work anymore, that it's time to improve. In fact, falling apart begins with the desire for something better or more satisfying. *It all begins with desire.*

What I've discovered (and perhaps you have, too) is that there is an inner presence that moves you along. When you pay attention to this inner creature, your natural guidance system continues to move you to new levels of love, intelligence, wealth, health, happiness, and self-expression. When you ignore its urging and deny your need to express yourself at higher levels, you encounter conflict, stress, and other forms of shutdown and resistance.

Shutdown occurs when we feel guilty about wanting to grow and take chances, about wanting to be it all and have it all, making these desires out to be wrong.

Forget your "pictures." Each of us has pictures and expectations of what an ideal life would be. We have expectations about how we and others should be ideally. It's as if we decided, "If I could be like that or have that, I'd be happy; I'd feel complete." You may have all the symbols of success, all the symbols of happiness, love, and wealth, but that's not it. Symbols are never the real thing. Symbols by themselves are like having the words to a song but not the music. We sell out our soul, our integrity, our very lives for symbols, only to find they aren't "it." When we let go of those inner pictures and expectations, we experience huge growth.

To truly live and have what you want requires that you *move into your experience rather than try to live in your symbols.* People argue about and get upset over the symbols not being right or the expectations not being fulfilled. It was my experience that as I gave up expectations and symbols, everything I hoped those symbols and expectations would bring me came to me. It requires an act of courage to shift from the familiar world of symbols to the world of new experiences and creative essence.

I know your major fear is that you'll lose what is important to you, maybe lose everything you've worked for. But you *can* move to a life of experience if you want; there is another way.

Be glad you've "had it up to here." "Fed up" is a good sign. Most people who reach "fed up" experience a major shift in their lives, provided they move on to the next level.

Those who are fed up but nevertheless tolerate it get sick, are miserable, and have to do more of whatever they do to dull the pain, hurt, and disappointment. Nothing is worse than being disappointed with life. Life should be a celebration.

Symbol-oriented people will say, "Life is not that easy." Symbol-oriented people are the first to put down celebration, love, openness, and peace. Their hurt is deep, and they are far from being the joy-filled, enthusiastic, and curious children they once were. The child had to be put away, but it is still there crying out to be heard and nurtured. Such people try to destroy the child within everyone with whom they come in contact. But this can be changed by an act of courage and will. Yes, you may "fall apart" temporarily as a result of that act of courage and will. Just keep in mind that paying attention to your inner self generates growth, and growth always involves falling away from the old into a fresh life.

The process of falling apart begins when you realize you want something different from what you now have, that you need or desire a different quality of life in some way. Perhaps you decide that you want to have a more intimate relationship with your husband or wife, and what happens first is anger, separateness, and even the desire not to be there anymore. Or you meet a new person who is truly alive, appreciative, and is vitally interesting to you, and this makes all your other relationships look like yesterday's warmed-over oatmeal.

"Falling Together"—In 5 Easy Steps

Life is trying to contribute to you, but that can only happen through your willingness to surrender to it. Of course you never know at the onset how it will turn out, except that it always will be better than you can imagine or expect. Every loss is a gain that is not yet recognized, for it really is not a loss, but a falling away, a starting afresh.

STEP 1—LETTING GO

The first step of falling together is a step into the unknown, where you are not in control. Healing requires letting go of sickness. You can't be sick and well at the same time.

Keep on going. What we each need to know and experience is that everything in the universe, including ourselves, is imbued with the qualities of the divine and the miraculous. To experience that as a reality requires that you step out into the unknown and trust—even when it looks like it's not working. Keep going, keep correcting, keep speaking your word, and keep practicing the principles. Mastery of anything requires that you first become a student; the mastery of life demands that to be all you can be, you must forever be a student and a practicing master. There is no limit. There is always more, even though this moment is sufficient and whole unto itself.

The moment you realize that you and your wife/husband can experience greater intimacy and pleasure together, the fears, doubts, and concerns that you have not previously communicated to one another surface to be dealt with. Many people say, "Forget it. It's not worth it. It just makes worry and causes trouble, so I'll just get by, cope, and tolerate where we are. After all, some couples are worse off than we are, and we have a very good life compared to most. Why be greedy? You can't have it all anyway!" That's a sell-out. Once you have felt the need to move to a new level of life, that need or desire must be expressed so you can move to the next step.

STEP 2—FALLING APART

The second step is the upset stage, the "it's all falling apart" stage. Right here is where it looks like you're losing it, so you'd better hurry and patch it up. The same thing is true if you go to a nutritionist or otherwise dramatically alter your eating habits to heal your body. You will go through a "healing crisis" and time of discomfort, even possible illness. The tendency is to think it's not working and to revert back to your old ways.

Don't go back to "the old way." Suppose you realize it doesn't work to strike your child and now your child is rebelling. The challenge is: Do I go back to the old way, or do I allow myself to look to new, more loving, nurturing, and nonmanipulative ways of communicating with my child to assist him or her to become responsible and capable? At this stage it may look like the child does nothing but test you and press you to see how far he or she can go until you give in and even go back to the old ways. The child also has an investment in the manipulative game of punishment. It takes time to break old habits.

Here are some of the signs and manifestations of the second step of falling together, which really is temporarily falling apart.

* You feel worse.

* You feel out of control.

* You are upset.

* You cry.

* Others cry, are upset, etc.

* Everything looks hopeless.

* You fear losing everything.

* Other people criticize you.

* Others threaten to leave you.

* Others play their control games with more determination.

* Nothing looks good.

* There is conflict and disagreement.

* You wonder where your motivation went.

* You don't feel loving or loved.

* You complain about everything.

* You feel inadequate.

* You feel controlled and trapped.

Out with the Old

Communication and telling the absolute truth are actually a major part of falling together. There is constant need in life to communicate, and I don't mean just talk, complain, yak, or dump. What worked yesterday was only a building block for today. It may be obsolete and not needed today. Yesterday's answers truly don't work today. Only today's answers to today's questions will satisfy. During this time there is a purging or a need for cleansing and purification.

Cleaning out the old is actually the action needed to allow the renewal process to do its work. This will mean giving up old habits of controlling others, not playing your parents' games, not feeling guilty for having what you want. This will mean actually moving out the old furniture and choosing what you really want. Here is where relationships that have never worked need to go—or at least the unworkable way in which the relationship was being created has to go. You can bring a long-term relationship totally to life by choosing that it be that way.

The Role of True Love

Love is not a feeling or an emotion, it is a context. For example, do you stop loving your child if he or she disappoints you or gets angry or messes in their pants? No, you live from the context of "I love my child." Within a pure context of love that you allow to be created through your declaration of that context, everything generates itself into love. Everything that happens is an opportunity to experience and express more love and greater intimacy, understanding, compassion, trust, and truth.

True love happens out of trust, commitment, and integrity. It becomes more empowering every day. It is a spiritually transformed relationship wherein your life is surrendered to the Holy Spirit and you transcend pettiness and ego.

Look to see what works. All relationships work when lived in the context of love. You may not want to continue or work with all of them. Some may have a long way to go and you don't want to invest the time. Other people may not choose to be committed to the same purpose or games in life as you. I gave up saving people a long time ago, when I almost died in the effort. There are plenty of conscious, alive, and committed people who want what you want. It's much easier to do the same dance together. We need to let go of what no longer works.

STEP 3—ADOPT A NEW PATTERN

The next step is now to do what works, to practice the new way. This can be awkward, because you are not an expert. You are a beginner. Keep on.

Learning to play tennis from an expert may foul up your tennis game until you have incorporated the new method into your self. You will make a lot of mistakes, have a lot of fear and doubts. Your results will tell you to go back to the old way, this isn't working. Keep on. There is a term for this, "going to the wall," which means giving your all and going to a new level. It's like weight lifting—you feel you can't go any further, but you make one last push to break through to the next level. Challenges look huge to me. I don't have answers, the old way doesn't work, and I don't know what to do. However, in looking at each challenge—examining it, asking questions as to what I know and what I need—right to the point of hopeless mental exhaustion and frustration, a light turns on and all is clear; the truth is known.

Place a real demand on yourself. This kind of opportunity places a demand on your inner resources *and* brings out of you everything you need or want. It's all within you. You have to work with yourself to bring it out. You must draw it out of yourself by placing a demand on it. The truth is you are actually restoring yourself. You can't have what you don't have. It doesn't come from anywhere outside of you; it is generated from within and brought forth through your effort. *It takes effort to seem to live effortlessly.*

If you meditate, you'll know what I'm saying. It's uncomfortable to sit and not do anything. You want to get up, eat, talk on the phone—anything but sit there and breathe. By remaining there, discomfort builds to an almost intolerable point. And then in a moment it's gone, and there is a deeply satisfying and highly pleasurable experience that continues to build. There always seems to be an uncomfortable part, but it gets smaller and smaller as you resist it less and less, so the process moves more quickly as you become friends with it. *Right on the other side of the most uncomfortable part is the breakthrough to a whole new level.*

If you keep at it, you will shift your three lower, animal, physical centers through your fourth, the heart or center, into your upper three levels of being and living.

Commit to do what it takes. In the Bible story of the prodigal son, the runaway son had to turn around in his weak, humbled state with every bit of strength that he had in order to move in the direction of his father's house— home. His father met him and showered him with gifts. That symbolizes to me that, until we realize that is not "it," we seek the lower pleasures and satisfaction of survival needs and think that's what life is about. We must turn ourselves into the healing space of God's love. Then we will rise into the pleasures and exhilaration of intelligence, intuition, imagination, and, above all, the ecstasy of God's love through the Holy Spirit. Instead of being pleasure seekers we will live from God's pleasures.

Discipline yourself. Discipline is the key. Without discipline you can't have commitment. Putting the emphasis on being comfortable and to taking it easy will kill you. (I'm not saying you should be a workaholic. That, too, will do you in, plus you'll drive everyone else around you to heart failure and high blood pressure.) I used to rebel at any sign of discipline. I believed it would rob me of my inner child and my job of living and what I called freedom. Yet now I find that *discipline has given me the freedom* for which I'd longed.

You move up by pressing through your resistance level into a higher state of being and living. *You are choosing either life or death.* If you are on the downswing, as most are, *you've got to get yourself up*, which probably means reversing and going in the opposite direction in every area of your life.

Just keep moving. Keep loving and forgiving yourself. Keep on keeping on. You may start a new nutritional program and then find yourself "pigging out" on ice cream. Great! Notice how you feel, what your body feels like, whether it satisfies you, etc. Forgive yourself and *begin again*. You are perfect exactly the way you are. The issue is not perfection. The issue is optimal living and full actualization of self through the energy of love. Nothing works without love. That's why all attempts to get better fail. *You can't get better. There is nothing wrong with you.* Total unconditional love for whatever whenever is the turning point and the only absolute transformer of your life. Love eternally flips you right side up and restores you to your rightful place.

Face life squarely. The main blockage that could keep you from allowing your life to fall together is the fear of disapproval or being wrong. To correct that, stop judging, or making anyone wrong, no matter who and what. Of course there are consequences. You speed and you get a speeding ticket. But don't use the ticket as an opportunity to judge or blame yourself, the policeman, or somebody else. *Just clean up your mess. Be responsible for it*, as must everyone. Don't use it as an excuse or opportunity for even a moment of judgment. Love, love, and keep loving.

Don't look back. You may at times feel a great desire to take back old stuff or to return to old beliefs because nothing has come along yet to take their place. The new relationship or whatever hasn't arrived as yet, even though you've declared what you want. The new clothes haven't shown up; the ones you threw away are still in the bag for Goodwill, and you are having second thoughts. *Don't go back.* Remember Lot's wife in the Old Testament. She looked back to a life of worthlessness and turned into a pillar of salt.

You can't go back. There is nothing worthwhile there.

STEP 4—ALLOW THE EMPTINESS

Allowing the emptiness. Don't hurry to fill it up. This is time for you to enjoy . . . to read and write . . . to be filled with ideas and truth. Take this time to learn what is available, open your eyes to a whole new level of living. Use this period to clearly realize and declare the whole new context, the whole new quality of your existence. Be open, refresh yourself—vacation, relax, restore, and be filled with love and truth.

STEP 5—ACCEPT THE INFLOW

Experience how the emptiness begins filling with a new life and a new way of being. It flows naturally like an inner fountain, meeting your needs and giving you your heart's desire. This is a time of exhilaration, of being on top of the world and being glad you are alive. Your life has fallen together. The exhilaration will last for a while, and then the process will begin again. But it will be less uncomfortable each time. You will become friends with yourself and master the inner learning that leads to your next growth opportunity. *Seek and ye shall find, knock and it shall be opened unto you, ask and ye shall receive.* Life works. Go with the flow that moves you to more life.

Exercises

Write the answers to these questions as well as the affirmations in your notebook or journal.

1. What are you trying to hold together and keep from falling apart?
   a. What do you use to keep these things together?
   b. What are your fears and beliefs about letting them go? List ten fears and ten beliefs.

2. Give up control, domination, and manipulation and allow people to be the way they are and the way they are not. Do it for an hour, then a day, a week, two weeks, etc.

3. What would happen if it all fell apart? What would happen after that? Keep answering this question until you laugh.

4. Where are you more committed to looking good, impressing other people, or proving you are a success than to being happy, alive, and doing what you want?

Affirmations

(*Write each one ten to twenty times a day until you have incorporated them into yourself.*)

I, _____, only lose what I don't want so that God's greater gift for me can be in my life.

I, _____, continually surrender my life to God through the Holy Spirit and allow everything to fall into its right place.

I, _____, let go of my attachments to concepts of how I think something should be and allow something better to come in.

Others' thoughts and judgments have nothing to do with me.

I, _____, give myself permission to live as I choose.

I, _____, trust God's love to take care of me and others.

* 16 *

People: Whom to Keep and Whom to Let Go

"Am I getting what I want in this relationship, and are you getting what you want in it?"

This is the key question to ask in each of your relationships. A relationship works as long as you *and* the other person get what you want. When you aren't getting what you want, it's time to take a look at what's going on. What worked yesterday may not work today; what didn't work yesterday may work today.

Love—the Gift of Grace

A fundamental truth about us is that we all love each other at some level of our beings. We actually adore and cherish each other and can and do love all people the same.

However, *being in love is not a good enough reason to be together in a partnership*. To love someone says nothing, for the truth is that you love everyone and everyone loves you, even if that doesn't appear to be true. Love is experienced when you make a heart connection, when nothing is wanted or expected. Then you are each perfectly acceptable as you are in each other's presence. *You each fall in love with yourself when you are with that other person.*

Love is the fundamental, absolute truth of life. It is all there is and all that we truly seek. It's ours right now— always has been and always will be. It defines who you are—you can be open to love or resistant to it. Judgment puts limits and restrictions on love. Love has nothing to do with limits or achievement; it can't be earned, deserved, or lost. It comes to all through the grace of God. *Grace* is a Biblical term meaning God's love for you beyond what you do or don't do. That love transcends this earth. You live by grace merely as a gift; truly something for nothing.

Consider these truths about love:

* *When we allow ourselves to love people, we are extending the gift of grace.*

* *Love is there when you surrender into love. Love can be there with another the moment you find something in common to talk about, find something to love or like about each other, and when you share of yourself through communication. Love naturally comes to the surface when the shell you use to separate yourself from others cracks open.*

GROUNDS FOR A RELATIONSHIP

Since love isn't grounds for anything but love, what is a relationship? *We're each in a relationship with everyone.*

We are related—we are truly one—with all life. Each of us is a mystic tapping into the wisdom and truth of the universe. Nothing is kept from you if you are willing to know it. You are in a relationship with all people, to say nothing of all other life forms.

* *You are already in a relationship even with people you don't know.*

* *Your close relationships are for a purpose.*

Yes, the people you are involved with in a more intimate relationship are there for a specific reason. Some of them are teachers, and you are restored to your power through the difficulty you experience with them. It is a learning experience. Some are purely lovers, providing close relationships where it takes no effort to understand and relate to one another.

Relationships can either be entanglements and destructive, or empowering and inspiring. What makes the difference? It is your awareness of your own purposes in life and your willingness to choose close relationships that support your purpose and vision.

I want to be clear about one thing: Even the most magnificent relationships embrace challenges and opportunities that look like crises. In fact each crisis is an opportunity to let go of separateness and to move into a more intimate experience of love.

If love isn't enough reason to be together, what is? This is what I've discovered, as I'm sure on some level you have, too: For a relationsip to be empowering, you must see a common purpose and be willing for the other person(s), as *well* as yourself, to win.

Look at Your Relationships

Write down the names and purpose of each of your meaningful relationships. Are you winning or losing in each?

I used to find myself out of step with others and wonder why. While I condemned myself for not being "enough" or the "right way," I constantly struggled to get the other person to follow my lead and live my way. It never worked; I lived in a constant state of emotional turmoil. I felt inadequate and saw my partners and coworkers as unwilling to appreciate me and go my way. There was a constant tug-of-war. It looked to me as if the way to win was to deny others my love, to blame them for not seeing the truth, and ultimately to disconnect out of anger or avoidance. I was confused. How could I love someone (which I did) and still have so much dissatisfaction?

The truth is I really never chose. Each person has the right to choose what they are up to in life. *See life for what it is.* Life is a game. That means you are constantly choosing what games you want to play, what steps you want to dance.

I remember being alone in my home one evening and feeling a deep yearning to relate to someone who could be a true soulmate. I talked to God—in my own way. Basically I said, "If you have a soulmate for me, bring him to me. If not, let me know and I will live your will. I know you couldn't give me a dream or desire without that already being mine. I want to be with my life partner and I'm willing to surrender to whatever that takes." It was shortly after that I met my husband-to-be, Leonard Radomile. He was everything my heart desired and more. What is so phenomenal is that we are one soul, opposite and the same, our love is the same. We bring different gifts to each other that contribute to us and expand our awareness and experiences. This is an example of the miracles that happen when I turn things over to God, who knows more about me than I am conscious of at any time.

This relationship was God's gift to me as I let go of a huge amount of fear in relationship with men, discovered how to love without demand, and when he and I went on from the marriage into a new form in our relationship, I experienced the letting go of what I had made more important than God. Each relationship is perfect, some for an instant and others for a lifetime. Each is a blessing.

What you deeply desire is already yours, waiting for your acceptance. *Commit to the opportunity*. Few people are committed to the opportunity that relationsips offer. Where the ego is in charge, love ebbs. Instead you have a compulsion to be "right" at any cost, even if it means admitting you are wrong so that you can prove how wrong *others are for making you wrong*, which makes you right. The ego-dominated relationship is an entanglement wherein no one wins.

Each of my relationships has been a learning experience. The lesson to me is always to tell the truth, to be myself, and to be true to my purpose and vision in life. If your vision is to be a gardener, do that. If your mate wants you to be a golf pro, it won't work if you don't want that for yourself. Let people go where they want to go. Go where you want to go, and find your partners in the group that's going in your direction.

ALIGNMENT OF PURPOSE

To choose to be in relationship with people who are going in your direction may seem like closing yourself off to many growth opportunities. It isn't. You can have many purposes and interests. You can play in all the games and win in all the games. You can be open to all you choose to be open to, and enjoy the quality of your relationships as empowering and inspiring. Alignment of purpose is necessary in relationships; it's misalignment that limits you. It doesn't matter what your purpose is. It could be:

* To have a loving, inspiring marriage that empowers others to have loving, inspiring marriages

* To end starvation in the world

* To win a boat race

* To produce a product that allows people to grow hair on their bald heads

* To bring heaven to earth

* To have children get the quality of education that allows them to be happy and successful in life

* To play and have fun

* To build airplanes that are safe and economical to fly while carrying two hundred passengers

Declare your purpose. See who is playing the same game and who isn't. Remember that actions speak louder than words. You may be up to a loving, spiritual marriage, while your mate is up to violence and suffering. You don't have to change your purpose, and neither does the other person. Simply look to see what you want and get on with it. Yes, that can mean letting go of a relationship that is blocking you.

As another example, you may own your business and want to build a transformed, nurturing, and profitable operation based on trust, integrity, commitment, service, and excellence. If that is what you want, tell your employees and let them choose whether that is also their purpose or not. After your declaration, you will be able to differentiate those who are with you from those who aren't.

LETTING GO IS NO BIG DEAL

We make letting go of people such a big deal; to justify moving on we create big hassles and dramas. You can love someone and not play the same game together. Love is not the basis for partnership; common purpose is the basis for partnership. Love is always there, no matter what. And there is no standard for a perfect relationship. The relationship merely needs to serve you and the other participants.

Love does not mean self-denial. The most painful thing I know is to deny yourself and your purpose in order to keep someone in your life. There is no scarcity of people on this earth. There are approximately 4.6 billion people in the world, and you are totally in love with each; you are related to each and one with each. You probably don't want to spend time with each. Some you don't even want to see, let alone be close to.

Choose your partners from people who are willing to have you win and be magnificent. Why choose people who want you to fail and lose? Each of us is a winner if we but claim that right. I can't make someone win if he or she doesn't want to. I used to choose mates, friends, and co-workers based on the potential I thought I could bring out in them. Yes, each of them improved the quality of their lives to some degree, but I was being dragged down and damaged in the process. I had low self-esteem and was afraid to be with winners, so I stayed with people with whom I could appear more powerful. I had a fear of rejection, so, to protect myself, I made sure that I was the one to give the good. I didn't ask to get anything. I began to notice that

I wasn't getting anything; I was being drained. I was also negated and repressed in the process. I realized I was sabotaging myself and that I had to connect with people I really wanted to be with and admired. I had to stop playing my savior game. No one was doing anything to me that I wasn't doing to myself.

LEVELS OF AWARENESS

There are levels of awareness, and you can recognize every one. We manifest the love of life on our way up. A person moving up the scale, as from octave to octave on a piano, becomes more alive, more creative, more able, more supportive, and more in touch with who they are spiritually, mentally, and physically. Everyone and everything is made better by your presence. People thrive, become healthy, and happy around you. You move upward into higher levels of excellence, love, wealth, and mastery in every aspect of life.

When people have been overcome by failures and damaged by other suppressive people, they get so stuck in their downward spiral that they aren't even aware that they have the power to change things. Everyone can turn around—no one is irremediably lost. But you can't do it for them. You can offer the opportunity, but *they* must take it.

Be careful. You could be the suppressor. You may believe that the only way to get others to improve and get on the right track is your way, and it isn't. You can test your belief by whether others pick up in your presence or drop down. What works for me is loving people and supporting them in their purpose. I ask them, "How can I support you, and what would you want that to be like?"

No one has the right to tell you what to do until you give them that power, such as a coach you hire to train you in a sport, your supervisor or boss at work, or anyone you have joined in an empowering relationship because you want them to teach you what you don't know or help you do your part in a project. Surrendering to another is always a conscious choice to let go of the ego. Only surrender by choice to someone you trust. To trust another is not to give up your responsibility and say, "Here, take care of me, because I can't take care of myself."

WHAT SUPPORTS YOU

Let's look at what does and doesn't support you in relationships. Be aware of your energy and the energy you feel in the presence of others. Go with people with whom sharing is a joy. Why bother with anything else? Work should be joyful, marriage should be joyful, government should be joyful, exercise should be joyful, your relationships to money and possessions should be joyful.

Ask yourself, "Is this a healthy, alive, loving, and nurturing relationship?" If yes and it supports you, continue if you choose to. If it isn't, what are you doing to yourself? Ask yourself, "Am I loving, supportive, nurturing, and empowering in this relationship?" Maybe you just need to give up trying to shape up someone else into your idea of an okay individual.

Each of us has our blind spots and our areas of difficulty. Those have to be worked through in any relationship. But if a person isn't willing to move into higher levels of awareness, love, and good with you, it's difficult to remain in relationship with him or her and keep moving on. To let a person go doesn't mean he or she is bad. It simply means you aren't traveling the same path. The other person doesn't have to change, and who says you need to sacrifice your purpose, goals, and intentions? Always give people the opportunity to choose the direction in which they want to go. If they are committed to the path you are on, you'll know because they'll choose that; if not, let them follow their own path and their own calling. You can't do anything else and flourish.

For a loving, purposeful relationship, here are some emotional levels to beware of and avoid in yourself and others. They are manifestations of being caught up in scarcity, fear, loss, anger, and lack of purpose.

SUPPRESSIVE ATTITUDES—THE PSYCHIC SAPPER

Staying in the past
"I'm unable and helpless."
"Poor me."
"You shouldn't do/want that."
Covertly hostile
Sarcastic
Emotional and physical abuser
Put-down artist
"I only want to help you."
"You look tired; let me take care of you."
"I'm here to save you and make you better."
"You can't do it right."
Constantly bored and boring
"I'm no good."
Name caller
Lacking respect for others' property or rights
Not interested in life
"Everyone's a loser."
Jeering
Gossiper
Liar
Bad-news carrier
Constant crisis
"Life is a struggle."

Below are the empowering attitudes of a person in love with life and willing to be responsible for the quality of his or her own life. The presence of such a person is a contribution to all.

EMPOWERING ATTITUDES

"You are able."
"You are great."
"I love you."
"You can do it, and I'll assist you if you want me to."
"I value you."
"I want you to win."
"How can I serve you?"
"How can I enrich your life?"
"Life is great."
"Thank you, God, for my life."
"I can have what I want, and so can you."
Sees the good in everything
Is willing to clean up his or her own life
Does what he or she says
Tells the truth

You probably see yourself in both lists, for a healthy person actually sometimes thinks he or she might be doing something wrong. The person who faults everyone else is the one who is in trouble. A healthy person can find value in everything and use it to improve life.

ARE YOU LIVING OR DYING?

Another question to ask yourself is, "Am I dying in this relationship, or am I really living?" In a committed, supportive relationship, each person is valued and each person's life is the prime and only consideration. A healthy relationship is a dynamic, not a state or destination; it is alive. When there are off-limit areas—sacred cows and forbidden emotions, questions, or experiences—the relationship has been given a death sentence, along with the people who create it. Total freedom to be, to express, and to communicate is a must. It's important to agree on ground rules for sharing.

I have friends who recently separated because their marriage had been based on the husband having sex with others and the wife accepting that because she wanted to be with him so much that she denied herself. The husband realized that his wife was dying in the relationship by denying her own purpose and wants. Now both are doing what they want, and they still love each other. She has a mate who wants a one-on-one relationship and loves her, and the husband has the relationships he chooses. Both are alive and continuing in their relationship with each other as friends, but not as husband and wife.

Why People Sell Out

What makes a person sell out in a relationship? Survival needs, money, "What-will-people-think?" "I can't take care of myself," "I'm too young," "I can't get a job," "We'll have to split the assets," low self-esteem, ignorance about the true value of living, and more. It all comes down to not realizing that you can *have* and that you are a creator of having. You get what you settle for. Go for all of life's glory and ecstasy.

Why be miserable? Why use your relationship to beat yourself up? Why deny your life?

Even in a loving relationship, you will be miserable, bored, angry, afraid, lonely, upset, and hostile some of the time. What you must do if you can is to communicate and tell the truth in a loving way. In a good relationship, love and partnership go hand in hand. If you have chosen to play the game of life together with your soulmate, you are surrendering into God's love through this relationship. Actually, every relationship belongs to God and is holy.

Ask yourself these and similar questions, and I'm sure you will know whether you're selling yourself out for or in a relationship:

* "If my current problems were dispensed with, would I choose to be in a relationship with this person(s)?"

* "Is this relationship working for me now?"

* "If I weren't concerned about what others think, what would I do in this relationship?"

* "Am I willing to give up looking and accept this person as the only one, and do whatever it takes to have a loving and empowering relationship with him or her?"

* "Does this person make me feel good about myself, and do I feel more alive and better off in his or her presence?"

* "What kind of relationship do I want, and what am I willing to do about it?"

* "Am I the kind of person I'd want to be married to, live with, be friends with, or work with? If not, what qualities do I need to nurture within myself?"

THE MOST IMPORTANT POINT

When you know it's time to let go, let go. And don't go back! Hanging on to what doesn't work because you are afraid there is nothing or no one else for you will be your downfall. Life goes to the courageous. If you want what you have, give your all to it and choose to be satisfied and happy. No one can make any decisions for you; your life will always be what you have accepted for yourself.

You must give up the payoff you get out of relationships that don't work.

However, realize also that what may appear to be a relationship falling apart may instead be your failing to create the opportunity to communicate, to tell the truth, and/or to let go of your fears of intimacy. You and your partner(s) may benefit from counseling, a seminar program, awareness training, or a spiritual leader.

How to Become a Master

To become a master of relationships requires that you commit yourself to letting go of negative, fear-based patterns and open yourself up to love and support, whatever that takes. It won't happen overnight, but don't worry—if you want it, you'll have it. I feel our love and togetherness as I'm writing this. I feel your deepest desires.

Giving up the payoffs in limiting relationships frees you from the past.

Remember, you can't make any mistakes—there aren't any. Who's counting errors? Not me! I know you are able and that you will do what you must to take care of you. When you are true to yourself, you cannot be false to anyone.

Look within yourself now. Know whom to let go of and bless on their way, and know whom you want to be with. Everyone contributes to you, just as you do to them. You'll discover what you need. You can be trusted to do what is right for you!

Exercises

1. List the names of the people around who you feel depressed, down, unloved, and unappreciated. What did you want from them in the first place?

2. List the people around who you feel valuable, able, loved, appreciated, and full of energy and vitality. What is the difference in your attitude to them that causes a difference in them, when you are with them?

3. List the ideal qualities you would like in your relationships in the major areas of your life.

4. For each difficult person, list the things about them that upset you. Then find the same things within yourself and forgive yourself for them. Be grateful to those others for bringing to your attention what you need to love yourself for.

5. Where and how do you use the excuse of other people being difficult in order to avoid taking responsibility for your own life and doing what you want? List up to twenty ways.

6. What are the ways in which you distance yourself from others, create drama and upset, make them wrong, and deny love and pleasure? List at least twenty ways.

7. List at least twenty ways in which you acknowledge others, love others, allow intimacy, inspire others, and allow pleasure.

Affirmations

Write these frequently.

I, _____, lovingly forgive my mother for everything.

I, _____, lovingly forgive my father for everything.

I, _____, lovingly forgive myself for everything.

I, _____, forgive (another's name) for hurting me and not appreciating me.

I, _____, see the value and beauty in every person I meet.

I, _____, forgive myself for hurting (another's name) and not appreciating him/her.

All my relationships are for love and healing.

I, _____, am released from all past relationships, now.

* 17 *

Intimacy and Passion: Male/Female Energy

Your relationships mirror where you are in the marriage between the male and female energies within yourself. Peace, passion, and love come about naturally when you are whole in your relationship with yourself. Conflict, dullness, fear, and separation are the result of an incomplete relationship with yourself. Separation means isolation, and if you are at odds with yourself, you cement that isolation. Unity restores you to love and completeness.

We cannot escape healing our own "inner marriage." The way out is the way through. Those who refuse to resolve the conflict between their feelings and needs and their intellect and aggression will eventually destroy themselves. Any desire to harm ourselves or another comes from a belief that we need to kill something within us. None of us can be fulfilled and at peace when we believe that there is something wrong with us. All disease, crime, war, poverty, and acts of violence against another are outward expressions of an inner impulse to destroy ourselves after having judged ourselves evil and inadequate. What we must give up is the belief that we are or ever have been evil or inadequate. Whatever the question, love is the answer. There is enough love available for everyone to live as royalty. There is a special place for each of us where we can contribute our gift of love and live in ever-expanding levels of self-expression.

A healing is happening to each of us personally at this very moment, in our relationships to family, organizations, and the world. This healing is restoring us to our natural state of well-being and wholeness. It is at the point of wholeness and completeness that we actually begin to live.

True living occurs spontaneously out of functioning naturally in harmony with yourself and the forces of the universe. When the majority of people on earth live naturally in tune with themselves and life, the energy and life that will be produced will be beyond our highest imagining.

Where Passion Comes From

Passion and violence come from the same energy. Passion is the result of love-directed energy. Violence is the result of fear-directed energy. Fear acted out is a statement of our own isolation and ignorance of who we are. Fear-motivated thoughts and action never create unity.

Wholeness generates passion. Passion is the ultimate sexual energy. It is the sense of being totally alive in every cell and atom of your being: it is being fully conscious, with all your senses highly aware and awake. It is experiencing deep and profound inner peace and merging yourself with the force of harmony in everything around you and beyond you.

Passion is the reward of living. Passion occurs when you live from and trust your feelings and intuition, when you have surrendered to your assertive nature and expressed your feelings out into life. Happy people know they can have what they want. An ideal relationship is one in which you say, "I want to be, do, or have such and such," and your mate either gives it to you or helps you get it. Check it out to see if fear surfaces from this observation. If it does, you need to take care of yourself. A loving and passionate relationship involves two whole people who trust their feelings and themselves and allow their assertive sides to back up how they feel and give them what they want.

Passionate people are lovers of life who fully express themselves on all levels. They act angry when they are angry; they act happy when they are happy; and they cry when they are sad. The great artists, musicians, writers, athletes, speakers, craftspeople, statespeople, innovators, and entrepreneurs live and create from that kind of honest passion. The vitality of their work is the outward expression of the vitality they feel.

Passion can only be generated out of intimacy and a complete release of control. You can release control only when you totally trust yourself and life. The more you trust yourself, the more your relationships manifest that trust, as does every part of your life.

Passion in Relationships

Let's deal with the creation of passion in relationships. You work out relationships with others just as you work out your relationship with yourself. The shift within creates a shift everywhere in your life. The more others do this also, the more we notice a shift in energy everywhere and experience love, wealth, health, happiness, and cooperation. That can happen in the least likely places with the least likely people. Heaven on earth is inevitable if only you make a commitment to it.

THE WAY IT'S BEEN

Women, as we've observed, traditionally have been the personification of feminine energy and men the personification of masculine energy. However, the feminine without the support of the masculine produces helplessness, bitchiness, anger, hostility (repressed, of course), and feelings of confusion, resentment, manipulation, and all the other so-called female traits that drive men crazy. Masculine energy, lacking its feminine complement, produces violence, hostility, rigid control, domination, inflexibility, insensitivity, coldness, and a lack of the ability to nurture.

When there is balance, with the feminine or feeling and intuitive energy leading and the masculine or assertive energy supporting, you have healthy, happy, alive, fulfilled, and loving people.

Nothing is more magnificent to a woman than a man who totally combines the best of both masculine and feminine traits. Nothing is more magnificent to a man than a woman who also combines both. The whole person has no harshness or conflict within him- or herself, for all their qualities of being have found a home and are at peace and in love with one another. Whole people attract whole people and have whole lives. Relationships are for the purpose of healing and restoring us to love. After the restoration, our lives together really begin.

CREATE A RELATIONSHIP DIALOGUE

How can you get in touch with your masculine and feminine aspects? Write out a description of your relationships and then look at this as a gauge of the balance between your masculine and feminine aspects. If you need a better balance, then consciously bring out and begin to express the quality that is being denied. Acknowledge, appreciate, and relax the side of yourself that is overcompensating, and watch the quality of your relationships change. You can't repress either energy. Both must exist and both are lovable.

I was totally confused about these aspects myself. Only recently have I finally come to terms with my feminine and masculine aspects and been able to allow the marriage and love relationship within myself to take place. It is a beautiful experience.

FORGET ROLE MODELS

No matter what you do for a living, there really aren't any role models for how you are supposed to be. You can be an auto mechanic and be soft, feeling, and nurturing and at the same time be mechanical, greasy, and able. A man can love to cook, arrange flowers, and clean house and still be strong, assertive, verbal, logical, and intellectual.

We no longer can afford to hurt ourselves by attaching a male body only to male energy or a female body only to feminine energy. No one can afford to turn off a part of themselves or to put their masculine in control. Your highest self, which directs you through your feelings and intuition, must be out in front, and it must be loving and childlike, playful and creative. Your masculine energy is there to protect and take care of your precious, beautiful self and to verbalize, back up, support, and express who you are out in the world.

THE POWER STRUGGLE

The power struggle in our relationships is a result of the fear of loss and the giving up of control. You can really only surrender to yourself, and only you can take care of you. As you do this, you will attract people who are safe to trust, fun to be with, and loving and able at the same time.

* *You will only attract what mirrors you.*

* *No one can harm you unless you are harming yourself first.*

* *No one can kill or destroy you if you haven't first killed and destroyed yourself.*

* *No one can steal from you if you haven't already stolen from yourself.*

* *No one can degrade you if you haven't already degraded yourself.*

* *No one can love you if you don't already love yourself.*

* *No one can give to you if you aren't already giving to yourself.*

Love and Nurture Yourself

It's amazing to me how I used to destroy my self-esteem to get the approval of a man, hoping he would appreciate me. It was impossible, for no one could have respected and approved of me more than I did myself. No one can give anything to you or take anything from you that you haven't already given to or taken from yourself. That's why you must love and nurture all of you, all of the time. Your inner self puts you in healing situations and always puts love in your life if you are willing to get the lesson and accept the love.

When I'm not okay with myself and I have negated my feelings, needs, or wants, or if I have negated my words, or behavior, all I can do to lift me up is to put you down. I will put you down for anything I would put myself down for, even though I may deny it and avoid telling the truth about it. Every judgment of another begins with your first making a judgment about yourself. You may judge another harshly for what you wouldn't allow yourself to do or for what you are doing already but refuse to acknowledge. Give up the judgment in either case. Forgive yourself, no matter what. See your feelings and needs as well as your behavior and words as okay. The more you accept yourself, all of yourself, the more you love and accept others.

Trust your feelings. Express yourself and allow others to do the same. When I repressed my feelings and looked for men to take care of me, I attracted men who withheld from me, just as I was withholding from myself. Now I experience that more and more loving men and women in my life give to me—nourish, respect, and care for me—because I'm doing that for myself. It's the same as the parable of the talents in the Bible. You get more of what you have. It's the law of increase.

Get involved with people and work through what's there to work with. Get into the thick of things, the heart of it. Remember, the way out is the way through.

SURRENDERING WORKS

To live with passion required a surrender to intimacy and an openness that few of us allow ourselves. You have nothing to lose and everything to gain. This means valuing yourself, trusting yourself, taking care of yourself, and asserting and expressing yourself, your ideas, and your feelings. It requires interaction and involvement. You can't be detached from people and attached to yourself.

Passionate living is letting go of the manipulative strings that we use to play out sick, unholy games. Whole people play the game of life for the ecstasy and aliveness. God is your source. You have it all, and you must accept that. When I didn't feel whole, I was afraid of my masculine energies; I was afraid I'd hurt the men I so loved and so resented. What I did was to withhold my power to make it easier for them, but it was hard on them and on me. False pretense doesn't work. It never has.

Where my passion is the greatest and where I've seen the marriage of my masculine and feminine create an unbeatable combination is in my public speaking. Something happens when I address a large group of people. I open myself to the intuitive flow of infinite wisdom within me and I own that gift by using my gifts of verbalization and behavior to express that wisdom. I am totally alive and out of this world. Charisma occurs. I am now bringing this marriage of energies into all areas of my life. Your energies relate perfectly when you experience and express your true self. When there is denial of this, all hell breaks loose. When there is reaffirmation of this, heaven is here once again.

Just imagine yourself being you to *the fullest* and say, "I love what I see in my mirror. My mirror reflects more beauty every day."

Exercises

1. Write a description of the way your main relationship appears at this time. Describe the relationship or the lack of one in as much detail as possible.

2. Visualize the male and the female in the relationship as both being you, and let this relationship become a dialogue with yourself between your feminine and masculine energies. Have them make an agreement to love and take care of each other and you.

3. Write down your ideal intimate relationship and include everything you desire this relationship to be. Withhold nothing, tell the truth, and express your deepest desires and needs.

4. List ten ways you deny your feminine nature. List ten fears you have in allowing your feminine nature to be fully expressed. Do this exercise for your masculine nature, also.

5. List the names of the men whom you were and are afraid of. List the names of the women whom you were and are afraid of. Look to see if you have repressed your own self-expression and how.

6. Find a safe way to express and release your anger and hurt having to do with men and women.

7. List the feminine and masculine qualities that you are now expressing comfortably.

8. What feelings and emotions do you find it difficult to pull up out of yourself and express? Give yourself permission to feel and express them more often until it's natural and easy for you.

9. When, where, and with whom do you find it difficult to ask for what you want and do what you feel like doing?

10. Recall the times in your life when you shut down and made a conscious decision not to feel or express your feelings and needs. Give yourself permission to open up.

11. Visualize yourself as a whole person expressing both your feminine and masculine energies fully and easily with yourself—in your relationships, in your work, and in your self-expression.

Affirmations

I, _____, am a loving, feeling, nurturing, and gentle person.

I, _____, am an intelligent, able, confident, and assertive person.

It's okay for me, _____, to experience passion and aliveness in my relationships.

I, _____, give myself permission to be a passionate, alive person all the time.

As I allow myself to be powerful, able, and vulnerable, I attract strong men who love me.

As I allow myself to be strong and vulnerable, I attract powerful and feminine women who love me.

****

The Sweet Life—Now

****

* 18 *

Transformation: What It Is and How to Get It

As he or she gets older, the untransformed person becomes worse off; the transformed person becomes better off. The transformed person has the direct experience of being a whole, loving, able being who causes or creates his or her own life in all its dimensions. The untransformed person believes himself/herself to be the effect or result of others, the past, luck, fate, life itself, and/or other forces in the world that are beyond control. Most people grow older but they don't grow up. Growing up or owning one's life is a challenge and one's greatest opportunity.

The good news is that you are responsible, but it doesn't always seem like or feel like the good news. I have fought being responsible almost my entire life, but becoming responsible is what has truly given me my life. By responsibility, I don't mean blame or guilt. To live your vision, to be, do, and have exactly what you want and to live a life of love, wealth and fulfillment, celebration and health require that you be responsible. The key is knowing that you are responsible for it all. This unlocks the door to everything you want. Getting it all requires that you first realize it is all yours to begin with. Ignorance of who you really are and of what is available to you is the obstacle that must be moved.

It's been said that knowing you have a problem is over half the solution. I'll add that awareness and willingness will do more than just solve your problems. They will allow you in effect to get back what you have given away. You can't have what you don't already have at some level. You can't want what isn't possible for you to have. You may say that you haven't given anything away, but *to be ignorant or unaware of what is available to you is just the same as giving it away.* You can't use or enjoy it. You can only waste what you don't use.

A wasted life is one in which the person holds self, love, talent, resources, and intelligence back from others and from life itself. The one who gives all gets all. The one who continuously discovers and takes back more of him- or herself and contributes that out into life receives all the rewards. What keeps every person from living as fully and magnificently as possible is the lack of awareness and willingness.

I remember that as a young married woman in my early twenties I wasn't very happy. My marriage was not loving and supportive, to say the least. Neither were the marriages of my friends. I didn't know marriage could be any different, because everywhere I looked I saw the same thing. It wasn't until I was miserable and my pain was intense that I began to say, "There must be more to life than this!" and to ask, "How can it be mine?" Life is about opening doors into *more life*! Some live as if in a prison, as if they have been sentenced to a lifetime of getting by, tolerating, suffering, putting up with, sacrificing, and self-denial. *No one but you denies you anything.* If you believe God denies you love, health, wealth, and happiness now, you've really got a challenge. You need to question your belief system. Spiritual ignorance is the worst kind of ignorance. Life is an abundant, loving, and joyous celebration every moment!

The sun shines on all alike—it's just that some have their backs to the light and are looking into the darkness. Darkness is all that they perceive, everywhere. To them I say, *Turn around!*

Each of us has denied ourself our power and our rights to some degree or other. Actually, we still have those powers and rights, but we must revitalize them. I see greatness and genius in every person. I admit that it is easier to spot in some than in others—some people are so damaged that there is barely a sign or flicker of life. The damage that has been done to the real down-and-outers is obvious, but there is damage in everyone, except for those rare individuals who have restored themselves and continue to restore themselves to their full power, abilities, wisdom, intelligence, and sanity. They see life as it truly is and are committed to love and life itself. Love of itself restores one fully. It heals the heart, soul, and body of anyone who is aware and willing enough to participate in it.

Know Who You Are

Many of us have forgotten who we are and that we can have it all. This book is written from the premise that you are whole, complete, and perfect and have the natural ability to create through your imagination or your reactive mind (where the problem lies). You are a healthy cell in the body of the universe. What is known in the grand-scale macrocosm (that what you need is within you—the resources are available, as are the knowledge and power) is knowable in the small-scale microcosm.

* *What is natural to you is wealth, love, wisdom, truth, health, full self-expression, and the wherewithal to turn your dreams, ideas, and plans into reality.*

* *Life is a game to be played full out, and there are rules, or universal laws, with consequences for playing by or against these rules.*

* *You get what you want by playing by the rules. It's much easier, and then it all works as it was meant to work. Not knowing or playing against the rules works in opposition and brings grave consequences.*

* *Ignorance of these rules is no excuse, just as life is not fair. The goodies go to those who claim them and play by the rules. Others miss out.*

* *Everyone plays and most are not winning. The object is for everyone to win, and everyone can. There is abundance for all. In fact, life can work fully only when everyone is winning.*

Throughout time, we have denied or forgotten who we are, and yet always deeply desired to be restored to ourselves. Man is asleep and in this state lives some form of nightmare. Just having the flu is a nightmare compared with radiant health. Certainly the nightmare of poverty or frustration at not making ends meet is very real. Many do not question their lot in life or, if they do, believe someone else is "doing it to them" in one way or another. The most important quality of life is love—it is all any of us is seeking, whether we are aware of it or not. The denial of love results in fear, the fear of loss. Loss gone far enough is death in some form or another. Love gone far enough is life fully being lived.

We are love. The damage we experience is the result of our forgetting that we are love and therefore feeling we are not much. We forget that we have the power over the conditions in our world and ignore the truth that our very ideas, notions, thoughts, and intentions actually make our world what it is. *You can't lose in life—it's all yours*. The crime, war, starvation, poverty, sickness, misery, and helplessness in our lives and in the world are the results of not knowing. Transformation is about knowing. I'm not saying it's easy, but the principles are simple. They require turning yourself around to turn life around. It's inevitable that you will wake up; it's happening now. There really isn't any choice. The question is *when*.

Choose to be who you are. Somewhere in time a shift occurred within each of us. Some of us are aware of it; others are not. That shift was about being fed up with the power struggle on this planet and deciding to stop playing that game. The consequences are not worth it. The game of the ego *robs* you of everything worthwhile, and it still requires your total commitment. Love *gives* you everything (and more than you ever dreamed of). It also requires your total commitment. The transformed person chooses the path of love and everything; the untransformed person chooses the path of the ego and loss *disguised* as everything.

You will find the steps to transformation, so far, in this

book. I say "so far" because there is always more to discover—what we know and experience today is but the foundation of tomorrow.

The experiment is for you to open yourself by putting the information and the exercises and techniques to work for you. Practice them in your daily life, then observe the results. This is a way of life, not a Band-aid.

The following is a favorite story of mine:

Once upon a time there were four men who set out to see their fortunes. They had heard there was a buried treasure on the other side of the forest, so they began their journey by stepping into the dark and shadowy woods.

The noises were strange and the forest seemed to move with strange animals and forms. The four men huddled together, inching their way through the trees. One of the men decided to turn back. He felt he had too much to lose. After all, on second thought, he really couldn't complain, because his life was just as good as the others' and even better than a few. He turned around and went back, while the other three continued on with the hope and the dream of a vast and wonderful treasure.

They came to a little old man who asked them where they were going. They told him and he said, "Yes, you are on the right path. You will be frightened by all kinds of animals now. In some ways it will be more terrifying than anything you have ever faced, but trust me. Do not stop, do not turn back, do not walk to either side. Stay on the path."

The three set out again. Now the sights, sounds, and smells were indeed more frightening than anything they had ever experienced before. Just when they were about to give up, there appeared a castle and a kingdom in the far distance. All three jumped up and down with joy and pleasure until they saw two ferocious lions right on the path. There was no way to go around or avoid the roaring lions. Two of the men, shaking with fear, said there was no treasure worthy of their lives and they turned around.

The last of the four remembered the little old man who said just to stay on the path and nothing would hurt him. With every bit of courage he had and with the vision and the dream in his heart, he proceeded once again along the path. The lions loomed larger and their roaring became louder and more savage, but he kept on walking, holding to the path one step after another, trusting all the while.

To his great surprise and delight, as he got close to the lions who appeared to be right on the path, he could see that they were chained to either side. There was room for him to walk through, and as he did, there was the kingdom with its gates fully open to welcome him.

This may be a fable, yet the message is clear. The rewards go to the visionaries, the courageous and the committed who are willing to risk. The story is a reminder that what you have been seeking is in that next step. I didn't have but the faintest hint of what my life would be like when I took my first step, but there was a force deep within me, ever so quiet but compelling, that drew me into this work and onto this path. The most exciting part of all of this is that where we are is always both the end and the beginning. There is always more to be discovered and experienced by taking that next step.

The Four Aspects of Transformation

RESPONSIBILITY

Transformation actually means restoring you to yourself or turning something into something else. An electrical transformer turns energy into power that can be used. Power is potential or kinetic, passive or active. Power can be used destructively or constructively. *Transformation happens when you experience a shift in your awareness.*

* *You now realize everything you have experienced in life has been generated out of you.*

* *You have become the point of the transformer. Life flows through you, and you can always have and always will be the one who determines how that power will be used, where it is directed, and the results it will produce.*

* *You are no longer a product of life, but the point between everything and nothing. At the same time, who you are holds and is all of it.*

* *You are the observer and the observed. You are one with all life everywhere.*

* *You used to say "look what happened to me," but now you say "look what happened through me." Life now becomes your mirror.*

* *The force of the universe funnels its energy through you. You either are true to yourself and allow that energy to create the life you want, or you don't.*

"Attacking" is a waste. A transformed person experiences life as a projection of him- or herself. It is no longer possible to say, "Look what that person did to me," without also saying, "Look what I did to me and that person." It may make interesting conversation over lunch to talk about what "he did" and what "you did" and what "isn't fair" or "right" about it all, but that doesn't empower you or anyone else. To attack or be attacked in any form or in any manner is a waste of human potential. One who attacks or is attacked has forgotten the power available to us. To wake up is to see clearly and to act from that. Guilt and blame have no place in responsibility. To wake up is to live beyond just getting by or surviving.

The choice is yours. To live at your optimal level in all areas of your life, first be a transformed person in the process of continual transformation. Live from "I am responsible," because you are. That means you are the cause of what is in your life; it is generated and projected out of you. You hold it all within the context of "I am a whole, able, loving, and creative being." Not to live your life in that context is to live it saying, "I am an incomplete, unable, unloving being who doesn't create." These are the choices. It's one or the other, and both require your total commitment.

RISK

The second aspect of transformation is your commitment to risk. Those who "go for it," whatever "it" is, and those who don't, are separated by the quality I call the courage—courage to step out into the unknown, to let go of whatever doesn't work anymore, and to *risk*. "Getting it all back" requires that you let go of or give up the imagined reward you gained by giving away your power in some form or other.

Surrender to not knowing. The ego always wants to separate you from love. Ask, "Am I committed to being happy or right?" Risk requires that you give up the comfort of self-righteousness. Not knowing and surrender put you in a high state of being. Ask yourself, "Am I committed to living fully or to being stuck?" Risking is rejecting what you don't want in favor of being out on the leading edge, continually stepping off into everything you *do* want. *The life you truly want requires everything you've got.* The Bible says you have to "die to be reborn." Risking can be frightening and bring up death fears. You've attached yourself to your beliefs, to possessions, to places, to values, and more. You are not these things.

Learn to let go. You have to let go of what you have to reach for and take what you want. It's actually a very natural flowing process when you're used to it. If you are not, it can be terrifying. You will get used to it and you will love it. Be prepared to have risk be a natural part of your life, if it isn't already (I don't mean live dangerously). The longer you wait for the "right time," for someone to "save you," or for a miracle to get rid of what you don't want without risking, the greater your fear and the less chance you will make it. Hope is the graveyard of dreams.

COMMITMENT

The third aspect of transformation is commitment. Nothing happens until you are committed. If you are waiting until it's all perfect—until you are certain and you know the outcome is certain—forget it. That experience happens only *after* you commit. Commitment is an existential act of courage. Most people haven't even committed to living!

Commitment isn't about "if it works out." It's about "It *does* work out, because I am responsible and I am committed!" Commitment isn't duty, obligation, struggle, or sacrifice. Ask yourself, "How committed am I?" It's our life. If *you* aren't committed, who is? I realize that many people want you to be more committed to them than they are to themselves. That doesn't work. That's a lose-lose game. It is commitment that allows you to have ecstasy, intensity, and love in relationship. It's the key to living at a level of magnificence, excellence, and wealth. It's all there for you, but it takes giving all of yourself. *The price of giving is receiving.*

Start where you are. The commitment you have to producing the results that you desire builds the momentum that enables you to operate at levels where you get back much more than you have put in. Many people who are afraid of commitment don't realize that they already are committed to something; it could be to life not working out for them. Commitment says, "You can count on me, I am one hundred percent responsible."

LOVE

The fourth aspect of transformation is love and spiritual transformation. Nothing happens without that, for there is no purpose to life without the essence of life. Life is a gift of love. To have it be anything else is a sin. Life is about trusting in a higher power, allowing existence to flow gently and laughing and playing all the way. This may sound ridiculous and unrealistic given the way the world looks now, but I'm not talking about the way it is and the way it's been. This is about the new world, the transformed world.

Love and work are both God's pleasure. My work is my pleasure, and pleasure is my work. Love is my life, and life is my love. The good things are here in this part. When the race is over, it's time to enjoy the winning. Being born is a winning ticket—collect your prize! There needs to be a shift in how you see life. It is either heaven or hell. And it is true; we can be in hell one minute and in heaven the next. It just takes shifting our allegiance and our perception.

Make a radical departure. A transformed world is not the old world patched up and redone. It's a new world where all things are made new. The new world isn't history repeating itself. It's about the end of war, end of crime, end of starvation, and the end of poverty and loneliness. To the average person this may seem unrealistic and impossible. That's because that person sees him- or herself as average. You are an ordinary person who does *extraordinary* things. In your natural state of well-being, life is a celebration. *There is nothing natural about being deprived.* Life is abundant and good. The question is, "How good are you *willing* for it to be?" Transformation is the next step. It requires that you begin by trusting yourself.

Your answers to your questions are within you.

Trusting yourself is an affirmation of trust in life. You have what it takes, and what it takes is getting it all back and using it. All you need do is restore yourself to whom and what you truly are.

Exercises

1. What am I unwilling to be responsible for creating or causing in my life?

2. Who is the cause of what happens in my life? To whom have I given my power, if not to God, through my own choices? List the names of the people and organizations.

3. What are the major barriers in your life at this time? List five ways to overcome each.

4. List the ten happiest and most joyous times in your life so far! Find ways to have joy and happiness be the *natural* way you live.

5. List five to ten ways you will create joy, happiness, and love in your life every day.

6. Write down ten to twenty ways in which you could share transformation with others.

7. Write down five ways in which you will be personally responsible for bringing God's love and wealth to yourself and to others.

Affirmations

I, _____, can do any and all things big and small through the power within me.

It's perfectly right for me, _____, to have everything I want.

The better my life, the greater is my contribution to others.

Everything I share comes back to me, _____, multiplied.

I, _____, am a whole, complete person.

* 19 *

Before We Say
Good-bye

This book brought me to new heights and depths of awareness. As this book has done its work on me, so it has on you. Our book, this organism called *How to Have More in a Have-Not World*, has a life of its own. It has transformed me again at new levels just as I know it has transformed your life again. I feel our closeness and our oneness, for we are on the same path with the same commitment to love, life, and the divine experiment. Before we say good-bye, there are a few last things that I want to share with you.

The first is that the only time in which you can live is in the moment. I'm sure you've heard me say that earlier and are aware that "this is where it's at." This is it, right here, right now. There is no other place, no other person, and no other time. Meditation allows you to be in the moment. Through your experience of the silence, the ecstasy, and pleasure of God's love, peace and wisdom spring forth into your consciousness and into every cell of your body. Find a system of meditation that allows you to be still and be with yourself. To just be and listen is awesome and profound.

Practice being in the moment—hear what you hear, see what you see, smell what you smell, touch what you touch, taste what you taste, and feel what you feel. Lie down and breathe in God's love and surrender, and the experience of the moment becomes the experience you long for. The more you allow yourself to be in the now, the more you are in the now. The more pleasure and happiness you allow yourself, the more pleasure and happiness you enjoy. To not be totally in the present moment is to be somewhere else and miss out on the goodies. To be in yesterday or tomorrow robs you of bliss. You can be at work and by fully being in the moment be in bliss and get your job done. If your job is planning the future, fully experience your body, your feelings, and yourself as the life force doing the job of planning the future.

A technique I use to be in the present is to be aware of my breathing. I consciously let go of tension and stress in my body as I fall into peace. Another technique I use is to dance, sing, or play the piano. Find what you love to do that absorbs all of you—something in which you lose yourself and become the experience.

Making love with your loved one requires you to be *there* and nowhere else, or you only have sex. Ecstasy can only be there sexually when you have surrendered into the love and the energy of your partner. Sex is then more than a release. It is a holy event where bodies are transcended.

Don't miss *this moment*; don't postpone what's available to you *this moment*. Move into it; let it own you, possess you, and consume you. To prepare and postpone is never to be ready. People postpone love, postpone happiness, postpone fun, and postpone doing what they want. "Tomorrow" is a disease of the mind. You laugh by laughing, you love by loving, and you enjoy by enjoying.

Look at what you value more than happiness, love, and pleasure. That is your God. Your terror keeps you postponing, planning, driving, waiting, and selling out your soul for a few coins. Give that up now, *this moment*. By living totally in the now, you are able to live every moment that comes. Nothing and no one can take away your joy and peace, because it's where you live.

To live fully is to give up the urge to die. You cannot live with death on the horizon. You cannot live with death as a companion. There is no death in the universe. All there is is life, ever changing and ever expressing itself in limitless forms and experiences. Let go of thinking about age and living in a time-set of seventy-five years. Life is about you experiencing more of yourself and more of God's infinite love forever. Give up the idea that to choose life is wrong, or bad.

I recall that in my giving up the death urge I was afraid that others would think I was strange or that they'd laugh at me for choosing life. Life isn't popular, and yet it's what everyone wants. The belief in death as a real event is common, so to let go of it as a fear may not sound possible. It isn't that we won't let go of these bodies at some time; it's that you cannot truly live when you entertain death. Death implies that God kills you and sets up the fear of living in people. To surrender to the moment requires that you surrender to life fully. Your only concern needs to be to living. You don't need to prepare for death. Don't prepare for harm, hurt, pain, or loss. You only make them real by preparing for them. They are ego-created illusions used to terrorize you and control others. Life is a blessing, not a curse. God isn't a murderer or a night-stalker who robs you of what you love. I know this may sound strange, but examine reality yourself and see the truth of it. Let go of your beliefs and thoughts about death. Become a hustler for aliveness. The worst thing that can happen is that you totally give up death as a reality, live fully, love life, and die. Guess what! You will have *lived*, and that's what's important! Stop postponing life!

Look to see where you have been denying yourself, postponing your life and giving power to the idea of death. To live for death is irresponsible, for you only use death as an escape hatch and a way to avoid cleaning up your life now. Give up death and tomorrow is an option. Live fully today and tomorrow will be today when it's here. Time and space are but aspects of the mind realm. Life is infinite, eternal, and all-consuming. Allow yourself to be consumed with the passion of *you being in this moment* and living as your only choice. Since life is the divine experiment, why not see where this one goes?

Ask yourself these questions:

* "What would life be like if death didn't exist?

* How could you live if you didn't have to get anywhere, earn a living, or improve yourself?

* What are you afraid will happen if you surrender into happiness, peace, and joy right this moment?

* What is more valuable to you than being totally alive, trusting yourself, and living in God's love?

Let nothing be more important than the quality of your living. It is the commitment you make to your life that will give you your life. The only way you can ever contribute to others is through your own example. You living love in the moment will inspire others also to live.

The second thought is about being kind and compassionate with yourself. I know I said it before, and I say it again. You may be like a newborn baby, emerging fragile and innocent as you shed layers of ignorance and lies. You may feel alone, as you've given up so much and the new isn't here as yet. But I am here, too, and there are thousands and millions more coming to join with you and give you strength. Much you must do alone. To be where you want to be, you must let go of where you are. You must walk the path alone, for it is in your aloneness that you will discover you have never been alone.

I've spent many lonely days and nights questioning, crying, and seeking and facing myself. It was all worth it. I just want you to know that I love you and life gets better each day. The process of falling apart is what creates the stress that pops you to a new level of life. You will continue to move into parts of yourself you were not loving before in order to love yourself more completely. Everything is there to provide an opportunity for you to trust yourself, to turn your life over to the Holy Spirit and accept more love and good. Remember that it all works for your good. The one who finds good in everything cannot be beaten. The investment you make in yourself is the one that pays off forever. I want you to keep going, tell the truth one more time, to clean up the mess one more time, to get out there again one more time, to forgive others one more time, and to choose love again one more time.

You are part of a growing culture of beings who this time are going to have it all and go even beyond that. Your courage to be who you are and live a life of love, wealth, and happiness inspires everyone. You are the one whom

God is using to restore earth to heaven. You are the one who must experience it first.

This book will only have worked for you or continue to work for you if you do what is asked and required. A tool you do not use is only potentially a tool. Refusing to use a key to unlock the door keeps you out of the house. Use this book. Use it over and over until you have transcended it as a tool. And besides using this book as a manual to have more of life in your life, share it with others. Turn others on to who they are and what their lives can be about. Give others the assist they may need to pull themselves up. Give them a copy of this book. I'll be sharing this message on television and radio over and over until our world is safe and loving for all people. I have my niche—where I can contribute—and so do you. Together we are more powerful.

I am here, and if you want to drop me a note and share of yourself, I'm available for that. Just know that we are together in our hearts. I know you love me just as I know that you know I love you. I believe in you, and I know you are able in every way. There isn't anything you can't be, do, or have with God as your source. This truly is the Good News. We'll meet somewhere and we'll know each other in our hearts. Let us keep our eyes open for others who are on the path, so that no matter how different we may appear to be, we can come together in our common purpose of love and peace. You are truly royalty in the kingdom of God, and I salute you. There is always more in store for you if you but claim it.

I love you,

Check any of the following boxes if you would like to receive additional information about Reverend Terry and her ministry and return it to:

Reverend Terry
P.O. Box 82138
San Diego, CA 92138

Or call 800–548–2600

- [ ] Classes in your area
- [ ] Books and tapes
- [ ] Home study courses
- [ ] Television program
- [ ] Prayer Ministry (Call 619/454–3015, a 24-hour hotline)
- [ ] Reverend Terry's monthly newsletter, *The Good News*

Name _____

Address _____

City _____ State _____ Zip _____

Phone Number _____

About the Author

Terry Cole-Whittaker reaches over half a million TV viewers weekly with her inspiring coast-to-coast Sunday television services. In addition, Terry Cole-Whittaker Ministries, in La Jolla, ministers to hundreds of thousands of persons annually, through its many outreach groups and services, which include classes, seminars, workshops, booklets, a newsletter, newspaper, phone counseling, audio tapes, and other activities. Ms. Cole-Whittaker's motivational talks are sought by many Fortune 500 companies, such as General Foods, Mobil, and Xerox. She makes her home in La Jolla, California.